JOY

COM   WITH THE

MORNING

JOY
COMES WITH THE
MORNING

The Positive Power
of Christian Encouragement

William M. Kinnaird

Stephen Ministries ■ St. Louis, Missouri

Joy Comes with the Morning

Published as part of the Care Classics® Series by Stephen Ministries. Copyright © 1994 by Stephen Ministries. All rights reserved. This edition licensed by permission of William M. Kinnaird. Previously published in 1979 by Abingdon.

ISBN 0-8499-2874-5
Library of Congress Catalog Card Number 79-6519
Printed in the United States of America.

13   11   09   07
 5   4   3   2

Weeping may linger for the night,
but joy comes with the morning.

Psalm 30:5

Dedication

I dedicated the first publication of this book to more than a dozen persons who especially loved and encouraged me when I so desperately needed that. And they were far from the only ones. Since then many more persons have done the same. I have experienced the truth of what John Donne wrote: "No man is an island." I know I never could have made it without those who have struggled with me. This book is dedicated to you. Without you this book wouldn't be possible. Thank you from the bottom of my heart.

Contents

Introduction *by Kenneth C. Haugk*   11

Foreword *by Paul Tournier*   13

Preface   15

Prologue: *Dark Night of the Soul*   17

Encouraging Ourselves

  1   The Surest Ego Builder   25

  2   An Experiment in Self-Love   28

  3   The Computer of Our Mind   31

  4   A Human Filtering System   35

  5   Heterosuggestion   39

  6   Take Off the Mask   43

  7   Vulnerability   47

  8   No-Knock Policy   49

  9   Family Communication   53

 10   Don't Judge Yourself   56

 11   Dying to Self   58

Encouraging Others

 12   Caring   63

 13   An Invitation to Live   66

 14   The Seeds of Love   69

 15   Altruism   71

 16   A Key to Mental Health   73

 17   Make My Garden Grow   75

 18   Affirming Gifts   77

19 Warts and All   79
20 Support   82
21 Acceptance   85
22 We Need Each Other   89
23 Hand in Hand   92
24 If I Were You   95
25 Special Glue   97
26 Friendship   99
27 Priesthood of All Believers   101
28 Charity Begins in the Home   104

God's Encouragement

29 Your Own Moon   109
30 Me Too, Dietrich   113
31 Each Person Has a Breaking Point   116
32 Rights   118
33 Major Disappointments   124
34 Failure   127
35 Don't Ever Give Up   130
36 Something to Hope For   133
37 Through the Eyes of Faith   135
38 Mid-Life Crisis   138
39 Does It Hurt to Be a Christian?   141
40 The Mark of Inner Healing   144
41 Can Reality Be Altered?   147
42 Past—That's What the Word Means   150

Epilogue: *Take Off the Black Robe*   153

Notes   156

Introduction

Have you ever prized a book over time, perhaps even regularly recommending it to friends, only to discover that it is out of print? Have you ever loaned a favorite book and then forgotten to whom you loaned it? When you went to buy another copy, you discovered to your dismay that it was out of print.

Stephen Ministries is giving new life to some well-loved books with its Care Classic® Series. Books in this series are high quality resources, theologically sound yet eminently practical and immediately applicable to daily living. They fill a definite need for individuals and congregations of all Christian denominations who are seeking quality resources to equip God's people for the work of ministry.

Joy Comes with the Morning, the first release in this series, has long been a favorite of mine. I first met Bill Kinnaird in 1982. I am impressed by his robust sense of humor and profound insights into the ministry of caring. The partnership between Bill and Stephen Ministries in republishing this excellent title gives many more readers the opportunity to learn and grow from his insights and honest sharing.

There is great depth to Bill Kinnaird's conversational style of writing. He has "been there" personally and is not afraid to talk about his experiences. This book can be used as a devotional resource and as a substantive spiritual guidebook. Bill tells the reader about Christian

11

caring and encouragement, both of which are integral elements in building a solid foundation for caring relationships. This generation—and every new generation—of Christian caring persons needs to read this book.

I hope this book empowers you spiritually, as it did me the first time I read it—and every time I read it again. I pray that the Holy Spirit will touch you and speak to you through the words of Bill Kinnaird.

Kenneth C. Haugk
Executive Director
Stephen Ministries

Foreword

Here is a book written out of love! This is what has touched me so poignantly. How much Bill Kinnaird loves his readers! I think that all his readers will feel it as I do. How he loves them in advance, if I may say so, even before this meeting which is the reading of his book. How he was awaiting them with love.

Really this book speaks for itself, and very personally. Readers will see the clear indication of the friendship which binds Bill Kinnaird and me together, and which we both felt so spontaneously when we first met in Austria. It is because of that that I am writing these lines, to express this friendship, and to convey that I myself, first of all, have discovered in this book the encouragement that he wants to communicate to his readers.

For me, not really knowledgeable in English, it was no small task to read from one end to the other, while constantly leafing through the dictionary, a whole book written in English. And yet, I did it without strain, with unflagging interest and pleasure, because it brought me so much incentive to live my faith. Love doesn't teach us about itself; it communicates itself to us. To read a book like this is not so much to learn something about love as to meet someone who loves us and who communicates his love to us.

What I always admire about Americans is their desire for progress, for personal development, and their indefatigable zeal in helping others to progress as well.

And to do it with such simplicity! Yes, what touches me so personally about Bill Kinnaird is this simplicity with which he writes. Love, in its essence, is so simple, and it is this which simplifies us.

Several times I have been asked to write a book about love. And I have always refused, saying that it was a subject too difficult for me. Yet, here it is, that book; and it is Bill Kinnaird who has written it. In reading it, I realize that if the subject seemed too difficult to me, it was because I was not able to be simple enough myself.

That which simplifies us, that which makes us really fit to love, is the personal encounter with Jesus Christ. It is in this that the author of this book gives us courage. What happens is that our meeting with him leads us on each page to the meeting with Jesus Christ. What a beautiful testimony to Jesus Christ!

Paul Tournier
Geneva
February 5, 1978

Preface

A friend of mine tells this story on himself. One day, in the full bloom of his youth, he visited Paul Tournier at the latter's home near Geneva, Switzerland.

My friend was full of vibrant enthusiasm about his Christian faith (as I sometimes tend to be). He had been traveling through Europe with two young college friends who were not as yet Christians, and he had been witnessing to them at every turn. He told Dr. Tournier of this, and Tournier, with all his wisdom and very much in character, replied: "Perhaps it would be better if you talked to them less and loved them more."

In this book all I can do is "talk." I wish you were here so I could "love you more." That is the *best* way to pass on Christianity, one to the other—perhaps the only way.

Prologue
Dark Night of the Soul

You've probably heard the expression "dark night of the soul," meaning a time of deep travail when all seems hopeless and useless, when the spirit is broken and to go on seems pointless, too excruciating. We just want to give up and die, even by our own hand if it can't be accomplished any other way. God's so-called presence and promises are of no help. We're too numbed and devastated to be encouraged by them.

Have you ever had a dark night of the soul? I have. I'd like to tell you I went through one (or two or three), came out, and never again visited the valley of despair. I'd like to tell you that all the chapters in this book were written after my dark night of the soul, that I never again entered the depths after experiencing Christ and his reality.

That wouldn't be so. After writing much of this book, after saying that Christ is the answer (he is!)—the *only* answer—and that he would bring us out of these dark nights of the soul (he will!), I went through one as bad as any I've ever experienced. I decided to mention this at the very beginning of the book. Somehow it just doesn't seem to fit in the middle, or even at the end. My story hasn't just begun; neither is it over.

That dark night of the soul was brought about by something that crushed me as deeply as anything ever could. I suppose I could beat around the bush or not identify it. But maybe it will help you more (the purpose of this book) if I come right out with it. It may not seem so painful to you if you haven't gone through it yourself. Even if you have, possibly you weren't as crushed as I was. But I'm sure many of you have gone through your own particular dark night of the soul, whether it be the loss of a child, a serious illness, unemployment, or whatever cruel circumstance of life that brought you despair. Mine was the remarriage of my ex-wife.

My divorce was not of my choosing. I had prayed for many years before it took place that the problems could be worked out. And I prayed for six years afterward that God would work a miracle. I went through many dark nights of the soul during those years. There were times when I didn't think I could make it. I wouldn't have had it not been for Jesus Christ and the beautiful people he sent to love and minister to me.

Somehow, though, during all that time, I never lost hope completely. I still believed Christ would touch the heart of my ex-wife, bringing her not only to a commitment of her life to him, but also a softening of her heart and a desire for reconciliation so our children could be raised in a home where Christ was the center and his lordship clearly evident. I bought into a concept stated by one minister I know: "The greatest gift you can give your children is a caring Christian home where the family shares and prays together."

I believed that was God's will for our family. Praying for our home to be restored was different from praying for a pink Cadillac or ten million dollars by breakfast tomorrow. Christ is so explicit in his stand *against* divorce and *for* love and reconciliation and forgiveness; I really believed I was in tune with the purposes of God and "abiding" in him and letting his words "abide" in me, as John 15:7 tells us to do. And the promise there is: "Ask what ye will, and it shall be done unto you" (KJV). I was asking for the reconciliation of our home as a loving Christian one.

It didn't happen. But I don't want to dwell on that. The hurt is too deep. What I want to tell you about is my struggle and Christ's victory. I questioned the Lord, especially about John 15:7 and Psalm 37 which says, "He shall give thee the desires of your heart," and "Commit thy way unto the Lord; trust also in him; and he shall bring it to pass" (KJV). A kindly head of an Anglican seminary in London appropriated that psalm for me and my family. It has been and still is my favorite psalm.

I knew the first question I would ask Christ when I saw him would be: "Were you misquoted? You said you would give me what I asked if I abided in you and let your words abide in me. I did that to the best of my human ability, fully realizing and acknowledging my imperfection. But it didn't happen. Why?"

I felt a trace of bitterness coming into my spirit until I realized again that anyone who would come down here and let himself be crucified on a cross wasn't the kind of person toward whom I could be bitter. He has already proven his character, which is one of great love, compassion, and caring.

I thought about a lot of other things, including my own witness. I had been proclaiming the goodness and the love of Christ for a long time. What did my own writings say to *me* in such a dark night of the soul? What would happen to my books if I ended the excruciating pain by my own hand? What would happen to the many people who (I hope) might be helped by them?

Then I thought of a very prominent minister who, after a beautiful career, had sunk into deep depression in his latter years. When I first heard of this some months back, I wondered, almost critically, "How could this be? How could this man fall into such deep despair?"

I thought of a woman in our church, a person of great faith, who discovered she had terminal cancer. The several times I went to see her in the hospital, she was just lying there, almost totally silent, with no trace of warmth or friendliness or a smile. I had learned from her family that she had taken the news very hard and had sunk into deep despair. I again wondered, almost critically, "How could this be? Isn't her faith worth anything? Shouldn't she even have a certain joy about going to be with the Lord?"

Then came this latest dark night of the soul, when I felt I would have traded places with her in an instant. I wanted out of this life. Death held no sting for me. It was a time during which many Christians could have chastised me, but most people didn't even know that my wife had remarried or that anything was wrong in my life. With them I was, as the lyrics of the old song go, "laughing on the outside, crying on the inside."

Ironically I had a letter from a friend in Washington, D.C., saying how joyous and enthusiastic my last letter had been and how happy I had seemed. I also heard from a dear friend in London and one extra-special friend in Louisville, Kentucky. She had known about the remarriage before I did, and wrote me that she had known I didn't know when we had talked on the phone, because of the "happy tone" in my voice. I only took off the mask with a few of my closest friends and pastors.

Do you know who helped me most at this time? Two friends—one, the woman in Louisville who wrote me, "You will experience anger, despair, and hurt. That is only normal." She understood! Bless her for saying that!

The other had gone through a similar experience. She told me that the day her husband remarried, she lay down on her bed and wept. She later lost her only child to leukemia. From what she said, she could really identify with me. She was sensitive to the hurt and pain I was experiencing. It wasn't a pity party. It was just a genuine understanding of another human being. I can't tell you how or why it helped. I can just tell you it did!

I once read something I think is appropriate here. I don't know the author, so I can't give him or her credit. I wish I could because what he or she says is so beautiful and meaningful and true: "In God's economy each person is given the key to unbind someone else, but never himself. That is the responsibility and ministry of another."

I'd like to tell you I now have the answer to John 15:7, that I've solved the riddle as to why we can do our best to abide in Christ and let him abide in us and still not have done unto us what we ask. I can't answer the same questions about Psalm 37. I don't know why I didn't get the desires of my heart. I don't know why

God didn't bring it to pass. I still think I'll ask him when I see him, not out of any bitterness, but just a genuine interest.

I'll tell you what I *do* know. I know Jesus Christ is real. I know he's there. I know he loves me. I know he knew what I was going through during my dark night of the soul. And I believe he isn't finished working in my life. I still believe Romans 8:28 is true, that he will work all things together for good. I think that's the most meaningful and helpful promise in the Bible. And I can identify with Peter who, when asked if he too were going to depart, answered, "Lord, to whom can we go? You have the words of eternal life" (John 6:68 NRSV).

I'm in the same situation. I don't have all the answers. But I have searched elsewhere and they aren't there either. They aren't to be found by leaving God and striking out on my own; I tried that once and failed miserably. I know the consciousness movements—the devotees of TM, yoga, Hare Krishna, and *est* don't have the answers. The occult doesn't. Only Jesus Christ does. And I'm putting all my hopes, all my dreams, all that I am or can be in his hands. As the beaver said to Susan in C. S. Lewis' *The Lion, the Witch, and the Wardrobe:* "'Course, He isn't safe. . . . But He's good. He's the King, I tell you."[1]

Are you in a dark night of the soul? Don't give up. I wish I were there to hug you and comfort you. I'd like to put my arm around you and say, as dear friends said to me, "I understand." Believe me, I do!

Encouraging Ourselves

For as he thinketh
in his heart, so is he.

Proverbs 23:7 (KJV)

1

The Surest
Ego Builder

This is a book about Christian encouragement. We need to encourage others, but we also need to be encouraged. Unless we feel good about ourselves, unless our ego is healthy, we can't help anybody else. We don't have anything to offer.

If you're anything like me, you get your greatest boost when something or someone makes you feel really worthwhile. And whether we own up to it or not, we're all human, and that means we need to have our egos boosted. None of us, no matter how much we may protest to the contrary, can make it without feeling worthwhile. In his popular book *I'm OK—You're OK*,[2] Thomas Harris says the healthy ego state is one in which we feel that we're okay and that others are also. Once we start feeling we're not okay, we're on the road to mental or emotional problems. So it makes sense to do things that cause us to feel we're worthwhile and to refrain from doing things that cause us to feel we're not.

You know what makes me feel the most worthwhile, the thing that gives my ego the greatest boost? It is when someone says, "Bill, you really helped me." That doesn't happen as often as it should, but when it does, I feel like a million dollars. I feel it's all worthwhile, even the suffering I may have gone through as a learning experience so I could be in a position to help that person.

One of my favorite expressions is "wounded healers," a phrase coined by Henri Nouwen. A wounded healer is somebody who has been wounded or gone through a great trial—emotional or physical—and who, because of that, has the understanding and empathy to help another.

In the strictest sense, none of us is a healer, but I do think the Lord uses us to help others. In fact, I think that is the way he most often helps others in need and answers their prayers. That has been true in my life. When I was most desperate and needed help, the Lord sent just the right person at the right time. And he has sent a lot of wounded healers to minister to me.

For a long time I wasn't able to minister to anybody else. I was too consumed with my own hurts. But now I can help someone with whose problems I can empathize because I've been there. And when that happens and the other person tells me about it, tells me that my life has meant something to him or her, then it is all worthwhile—every ounce of suffering, every fragment of pain.

One of my favorite Bible verses is Romans 8:28, which says that all things, even the bad things, work together for good for those who love God. I think that means he can take all the suffering and hurt and make a wounded healer out of each of us. He can use all those experiences, no matter how dreadful they may have been, for good to help others. Remember, if we hadn't gone through the bad times, we would not be able to help other people because we wouldn't be able to relate to them on the same level. And when we can relate and help, we feel okay.

2

An Experiment
in Self-Love

I'm trying a new experiment. It's difficult to know
yet just how it will turn out, but for the first time in my
life, I'm trying to consciously love myself.

We've all heard that we are to "love thy neighbor as
thyself." Unfortunately, loving others has been given
greater emphasis in the Christian church than loving
ourselves. In fact, I believe it has been emphasized to an
extreme our Lord never intended. Some of us have got-
ten the distorted notion that we have to wear hair shirts
and *hate* ourselves, or at least consider ourselves noth-
ings, before we can properly, unselfishly love another.
This may be somewhat of an exaggeration, but at least
some Christian teaching has stressed the idea that we
should be doormats and let other people walk all over
us. To be Christian we should care nothing for ourselves,
only for other people.

In recent years, though, there has been a wise and
helpful shift of emphasis to an acceptance of an old
truth that, before we can properly love another person,
we must love ourselves first. This was precisely what

Jesus was talking about in Matthew 22:39: "You shall love your neighbor as yourself."

I've come to firmly believe that it is impossible to love anyone else if we hate ourselves. Some way or another, that self-hatred will produce undue criticism or condemnation. It is impossible for people who hate themselves to be happy, and I don't believe unhappy people can love.

I have accepted this idea intellectually for many years, but I am now coming to new understanding of what it can mean in my life. I once listened carefully to a talk on the importance of self-esteem by a clinical psychologist. Several hours later the thought came to me (was it the work of the Holy Spirit?) that I should *consciously* try to love myself, not just give lip service to it, not just agree that it makes sense and stop there. I decided to start an experiment, and that's what I'm writing about here.

I know I am capable of loving deeply. I have two daughters I absolutely adore. They aren't perfect—who is? They have some faults I dislike, but that doesn't stop my loving them unconditionally. I try consciously to look at and think about and dwell on their good points, of which they have so many. Each one has some unique qualities of her own that I especially love. Once I wrote each of them a poem, emphasizing those special qualities that so endeared them to me. I tried to tell them it is who they are that I love, not what they do.

Then I started thinking—suppose I loved myself unconditionally like that. Suppose I dwelled on my good points and tried not to condemn myself for my faults. Suppose I forgave myself my mistakes as I forgive others theirs. There is nothing narcissistic or self-indulgent about this kind of self-love. Rather, it means that I look at myself objectively as another child of God.

How can we discriminate against ourselves? How can we refuse to love any child of God, even ourself? Jesus also told us to love our enemies, and with so many of us our greatest enemy is ourself. Think about that for a minute. How many times have you been your own worst enemy? How many times have you been almost totally self-destructive?

As I write this, I've only been at my experiment a short time, but so far I'm very comfortable with it. I'm coming to love myself for some qualities I have and to say "so what!" to others I've felt less desirable. That doesn't mean to say I'm refusing to change in those less desirable areas. But I'm saying to the Lord, "Okay, you know all about that. You love me anyway, so I'm going to love myself too, even in those areas. If you want to change me, I'm completely open to that. I'll cooperate with you. But I'm not going to get all uptight if I can't, by willpower, change the habits of a lifetime overnight."

3

The Computer
of Our Mind

I once attended a retreat called "Effective Living." The purpose was to show how we can reprogram our subconscious minds, how we can put positive thoughts into them instead of the negatives put there in early childhood and later by ourselves and the significant others in our lives.

Frankly, I was a little skeptical. I had read most of the positive thinking books going back to Norman Vincent Peale's classic, *The Power of Positive Thinking,* and continuing on with psychocybernetics and other how-to positive thought manuals.

It wasn't that I disagreed with what these books were saying. I just didn't think they were spiritual enough. I felt they left Christ out of the picture and placed the emphasis on our own efforts. I also felt a lot of them were "get-rich-quick" gimmicks: All we had to do was believe we were going to be wealthy, and in no time flat we'd be driving expensive cars and living in mansions.

Although I believe with all my heart that Christ's

message about "abundant living" wasn't just limited to spiritual things, I didn't think he was preaching a "chicken in every pot" and a filled-up two-car garage for everybody, either. I felt when we concentrated so much on the material aspects, we let the spiritual go by the board. I still feel that way, and I cringe when I see one of those books saying we are King's kids and should be rich materially.

This retreat, though, was different. The instructor explained how our minds act as computers—God-given computers. He further explained that God can use our mind-computers, for our good—even material good. Just as there is a cause and effect in computer programming, the same is true in our minds.

If we think in our conscious thoughts that we are no good and unworthy, our subconscious is going to get that message, accept it as valid, and influence our actions and lives in negative ways in keeping with this negative self-image. Similarly, if we feed the subconscious positive thoughts, thoughts saying we are okay, then the feedback will be positive. Again I'm not saying this is anything revolutionary. It isn't. Yet in the way I'm approaching it now, it's revolutionary for me.

In the last chapter I mentioned experimenting with a new kind of self-love, a love that would cause me consciously to think loving and good thoughts about myself as I do about those significant others who mean so very much to me. The experiment is working. I'm acknowledging now that Christ can use my subconscious to help me, that I can best cooperate with that help by committing my subconscious to him, just as I have the rest of my life. And I'm saying that it is only common sense to go along with what so many psychologists have discovered—namely that if we put negative thoughts into our minds, we're playing with fire. We are not cooperating with God. In a way, we are even "tempting" God by saying in effect, "Okay, I'll put in garbage and you bring out a fruit salad." Wouldn't it be cooperating more to give him the ingredients for a fruit salad and then let him put it together and dish it up?

Like any computer, our subconscious can only work with the information that it is given. These computer-minds of ours are so much more amazing than even the most gigantic computers. In some way our computer-minds can even bring about self-fulfilling prophecies. Proverbs 23:7 (KJV) says: "For as [a man] thinketh . . . so *is* he." And Christ told us that if we could believe certain things and pray, believing that we already have them, we would receive them. In another context he said that thinking about immoral things was just as much a sin as actually committing them. So there's excellent precedent in scripture for believing that our subconscious minds are extremely powerful and influential in what happens to us.

By what means then can I begin the process of reprogramming my mind? It all came clear to me at the retreat. We learned there the power of affirmations—writing out positive things like "I like myself unconditionally," and then meditating on that in the morning and evening with a mental picture of something positive about ourselves, like a warm letter from a dear friend with some real words of affirmation and encouragement. It's also saying, "I never devalue myself with destructive criticism."

As we feed our minds such positive thoughts as "I can do all things through Christ," the negatives will be gradually displaced. They aren't compatible with the positive programming that has consciously been placed in the subconscious.

Remember God loves you. Love yourself. Think positive thoughts about yourself, and put all your trust in him who will never fail you. Believe in your heart that Psalm 37:4-5 (KJV) is true: "Delight thyself also in the Lord; and he shall give thee the desires of thine heart. Commit thy way unto the Lord; trust also in him; and he shall bring it to pass."

4

A Human
Filtering System

I heard a discussion recently on bitterness and how it can act as a filtering system that colors all we think and feel about another person. The whole discussion was actually on meditation, but not the kind in which we try to empty our minds and then let whatever thoughts that will come into them. That's as far from Christian meditation as it could possibly be. In Christian meditation we do not empty our minds but, on the contrary, concentrate specifically on certain things—most usually passages of scripture—and ask the Holy Spirit to enlighten us and show us the meaning or what he wants us to learn, or how he wants to use this to guide us.

As opposed to this healthy meditation, there is an unhealthy kind where we continually think about or meditate on, for example, a grievance we have toward another. If we let ourselves dwell on an injustice done to us by another, even though it may have been perpetrated years ago, the subconscious mind is going to be contaminated by it and will act as a filtering system. Whatever good we hear about this other person is going to be colored by the bitterness that is now rooted in us. The bitterness filters out the good. It's as if we played a tape over and over that says, "John Smith is no good; John Smith hurt me." If we continue doing this, we're going to reach a stage where no matter what John Smith does, it can't look good to us. We're determined to find an ulterior motive in almost anything he does. The whole world may think John Smith is a great person, maybe even a changed person, but our subconscious mind is so powerful it will never let us accept that. We still won't be able to see any change or any good.

What's the antidote? I use the word *antidote* because these sicknesses of the personality, these grudges we hold against one another, these unforgiving attitudes are poisons. They poison our whole system or personality and eventually they are going to take their awful toll, just as any poison does. And they certainly poison relationships.

I know of an "anti-antidote," one sure method for *keeping* the poison. That's the rehashing of old injuries. I know of one woman who absolutely refused to forgive hurts (some real, some imagined) going back ten or more years. She willingly clung to them like prized possessions. Then she found a therapist who encouraged her to rehash these every week. The best advice she ever got was from a friend who told her to "quit going down there every week and dwelling on all of John's bad points. Look at him every morning and think of all the good things about him."

She refused to take the advice and the marriage

ended in divorce. She had played the bitterness tapes too long. They had so conditioned her filtering system that she could only see the bad in her husband. She never looked for the good.

I heard of another woman who went to see a different kind of therapist—a much wiser one. She was using as an excuse for her inability to relate to her husband the fact that her father had abused her when she was a child. Their dialogue went like this:

Doctor: "Is your father still alive?"

Patient: "No."

Doctor: "Oh, how long has he been dead?"

Patient: "Ten years."

Doctor: "Is he beating you now?"

Patient: "No, but . . ."

Doctor: "Oh, yes, he is. You're making him beat you so you can use that as an excuse for not relating to your husband."

Oh, how we use *past* hurts as *present* excuses for not relating to people. We continue to carry the grudges of poison and play over and over the tapes that tell us, "It's all his fault," "I'm not to blame," "I took no part in it," "He could never change, and I don't have to," "It's too late," and on and on ad nauseam. How much easier it is to blame the other person than to face up to our own responsibility and say, "I'm sorry too. Let's give it another chance," "Sure, I can forgive you. How can I do otherwise when I've been told we must forgive seventy times seven."

How about purifying our filtering systems starting today? How about looking for the good in others, especially those with whom we are having difficulties, and most certainly if they are in our own family? Wake up every morning, look over at the other person, and jot down a list of all the good things you can think about him or her. It might surprise you. Make it a challenge to discover new traits you never realized were there. And if you have a list of bad things, even if they're just in your mind, burn up the list and don't start another. Erase the negative tapes that keep playing in your mind. Maybe your new filtering system can't be developed overnight, but it can be built. The right kind of meditation will pave the way for a new life.

5

Heterosuggestion

The title for this chapter came to me from a book by Joseph Murphy, *The Power of Your Subconscious Mind.* Heterosuggestion, in the simplest of terms, means those suggestions coming from another person and bombarding our minds and thought processes. As Dr. Murphy explains it:

> In its constructive form, it is wonderful and magnificent. In its negative aspects, it is one of the most destructive of all the response patterns of the mind, resulting in patterns of misery, failure, suffering, sickness, and disaster.
>
> From infancy on, the majority of us have been given many negative suggestions. Not knowing how to thwart them, we unconsciously accepted them. Here are some of the negative suggestions: "You can't." "You'll never amount to anything." "You'll fail." "You haven't got a chance." "You're all wrong." "It's no use." . . . [and his list goes on]. Such impressions made on you cause behavior patterns that cause failure in your personal and social life.[3]

I know a man who is a classic illustration of what Murphy writes about. He was so conditioned by his wife to think he was a failure that he thought seriously about committing suicide. He would have except for some deeply committed Christians who loved him back to health and helped give him a feeling of self-worth. His wife had told him, "I'm embarrassed because you're a nobody," and had compared him unfavorably with other men she knew and wished he were like. This man bought the whole bit—hook, line, and sinker. He thought he was worthless. His subconscious mind couldn't sort out what was true and what was false. The subconscious mind is like that. As we saw in an earlier chapter, it receives and stores and acts on the data it is given just like any computer. Tell it that it is a "nobody," and "nobody" actions come forth. But tell it that it is a "somebody," and "somebody" actions begin to emerge.

Murphy offers an antidote to the poison of critical heterosuggestion. He calls it "autosuggestion," the continual telling yourself that you are okay, that you are a "somebody." I'm trying to do that in my own life. But I think there's perhaps an even better antidote. Unfortunately it isn't something you can do to or for yourself as you can in autosuggestion.

On the surface what I'm going to suggest now may not seem at first to be of direct help to you, but it certainly will help others—especially those significant others in your life for whom you committed to care. Knowing how devastating negative heterosuggestions can be, will you try positive heterosuggestion, which

Joseph Murphy says can be "wonderful and magnificent"? Instead of telling your husband or wife or child or acquaintance that you're embarrassed because they're a nobody, look for something good in them, and tell them about that. Tell them they're a somebody. And being a "somebody" doesn't, or shouldn't, depend on what they do, only on who they are. They don't have to be president of General Motors or Mrs. America to be somebody. They are already somebody in God's eyes. He makes no differentiation in his love between the most influential person or the meekest, between the most powerful and the most inept. No, by God's enabling love, he calls us to be all that we *can* be, which is so much more than most of us dream since we are conditioned by negative stimuli.

C. S. Lewis, in one of his superb masterworks, *The Screwtape Letters*, has Screwtape, a major devil in the pits, writing to his nephew Wormwood, who is on earth trying to win a human away from Christ. Screwtape tells Wormwood he has blown it by allowing the human to experience his uniqueness and self-worth. (Bear in mind the "enemy" he is writing about is Christ.)

As a preliminary to detaching him from the Enemy, you wanted to detach him from himself, and had made some progress in doing so. Now, all that is undone.

Of course I know that the Enemy also wants to detach men from themselves, but in a different way. Remember, always, that He really likes the little vermin, and *sets an absurd value on the distinctness of every one of them* [emphasis added]. When He talks of their losing their selves, He means only abandoning the clamor of self will; once they have done that, He really gives them back all their personality, and boasts (I am afraid, sincerely) that when they are wholly His, they will be more themselves than ever.[4]

Isn't that beautiful? It's typical C. S. Lewis. God is sincere in telling us that when we are his, we will be more ourselves than ever. All of our potential greatness is loosed by God's freeing love. We are children of God—made in his image and free once and for all from life's negatives and put-downs.

6

Take Off
the Mask

A healthy specimen of a man went to see a doctor because he was extremely depressed. The doctor examined him and found his physical condition to be absolutely perfect. He said to the man, "There's a circus in town with a marvelous clown by the name of Grimaldi. Everybody who goes to see him laughs. Why don't you do the same thing? He'll make you laugh and then you will feel better." The patient replied, "Doctor, I am Grimaldi!"

I guess a lot of us are Grimaldis. Many of us go through mental hell trying to project an image of something we aren't. John Powell has a term for that. He calls it "wearing a mask." In his book *Why Am I Afraid to Tell You Who I Am?*,[5] he says we shouldn't be afraid to take off the mask, to let the other person see what we're really like under all those layers we put on to impress others (or ourselves). Down deep there might be something even better—the real person, not just a facade we put on for the public, or our wife, or the boss, or our colleagues at the office. If we give them a chance to get to know who we really are, we might be surprised. We might find they like the real person even better than the phony one we have been parading around all these years. It is even possible we might end up liking ourselves.

There's another good reason for "taking off the mask." Wise counselors and authors are telling us of the dangers of covering up and suppressing our emotions. John Powell is one of these.

According to a book I read, one of the famous figures involved in the Watergate cover-up, a U.S. political scandal of the 1970s, thought he had to submerge his true feelings at any cost. At a young age he decided that he would have to keep his emotions suppressed and expose only what he felt others wanted or expected of him. Suppose a young man with these kinds of fears came in for counseling with John Powell. After empathically sizing up the situation, Father Powell (or any wise counselor) might say to him:

"Don't be afraid to be yourself. Don't be afraid to let others see you as you really are. Where in the world did you ever get the idea that you should hide your emotions? Young man, that is the worst possible thing you could do! All you will do is create tension that may at times become unbearable. You will never be able to develop any close, trusting relationships, for no one will ever be able to discover the real you. They'll never have a chance to know whether they like you or not. You'll end up with obsessions and hostilities you won't be able to deal with. You'll think everybody is against you, and you will be looking for enemies under every rock. Worst of all, you'll never be able to truly love. You'll be so worried someone will discover the real you that all your energies will be consumed in a cover-up."

Among the beautiful and wise things Jesus said is: "You will know the truth and the truth will make you free" (John 8:32 NRSV). I'm sure this can be applied in many ways, but an application that speaks to me is that we are always to be honest with ourselves and others about who we really are. If we know that truth and let others see it, we've got a good start on the road to freedom.

I'm *not* advocating we go around all the time with long faces, telling everybody we meet how depressed we are and what an awful day it is. That's going from the sublime to the ridiculous; it's just as bad as being a stoic and thinking we can gut everything out by self-discipline and self-sufficiency. Besides, if we do that we just may run off the few friends we have left!

The important thing is, to be human we must be able to admit our faults and failings. We must not be afraid to say "I was wrong," or "I'm sorry," or "I'm afraid," or "I hurt"—and especially not be too inhibited to say "I love you."

Ironically, people who can come to grips with their own inadequacies and limitations frequently are more effective in caring for and supporting others. I once received a letter from a friend saying, "Caring and supportive people need some degree of recognition (the more the better) of their own limitations and acceptance (not approval) of these, which enables them to accept others."

When we accept ourselves as we are and are free to open ourselves up to others, the dynamic for change has been set in motion. We can become all we are meant to be. We can be a support for others without having to judge them. We are not placed on this earth to see through each other, but to see each other through.

The letter from my friend also contained this insight:

> People can't fight my battles, nor make my deci-
> sions, but they can hold me up. They can com-
> fort me, reassure me, cheer me on. So many of
> our battles have to be fought essentially alone.
> But it is nice to know there is a cheering section
> close by, believing in me.

As we open ourselves up to others, we discover that we do indeed have quite a cheering section. I once attended a conference of European doctors concerned with helping people become whole persons. The keynote speaker said, "Becoming a person is loving and being loved by somebody." But before anybody can truly *love* us, they have to *know* us. Before they can be in our cheering section, they have to know for whom they are cheering. The only way to let that happen is to avoid the cover-ups.

7

Vulnerability

I believe in sharing, in being open and vulnerable with people. For me, learning to do this has been very therapeutic. I've been able to vent my emotions. I've been able to get them off my chest. A repressed or suppressed emotion is a poison. I think one of the reasons I've survived some rather serious emotional crises in my life is that I've been able to let out pent-up emotions. I've been very much the ulcer type much of my life, yet never had one. I suspect that facing and letting out my emotions has something to do with it.

A bulletin of the Christian Association for Psychological Studies contained an interesting article on being open with others. It is called "Intimacy and Spiritual Growth"[6] and was written by Clark Barshinger.

He defines intimacy as the ability to let ourselves be known by others. He believes God's most common means of speaking to us is through other people. In his article Barshinger says:

> The way to come to know ourselves is to become known by others. When I allow you to see

me in more transparent glimpses than I usually allow, I also come to see and better understand myself. . . . I come to respect my own courage to let you see what is really there. . . . It takes courage to allow myself to be exposed to your good will when I do not know if I am strong enough to defend myself against your misuse of my vulnerability.

He then talks about the profound healing that can take place when he opens his wounds, pains, and fears to the loving touch of another:

If I back away from letting you see me because I am afraid of seeing myself, I will indeed not see myself. . . .

So to grow toward a greater intimacy with my own self, I must be able to risk intimacy with you. And I have no doubt that this is fundamentally a spiritual journey. As a general rule, the arms God uses for holding me are yours. . . . I am overwhelmed with love when I sense you have seen even that part of me of which I am ashamed, you continue to approach me.

I have been loved and accepted like that. I have been held in the arms God uses for holding up the bleeding and wounded of the world. It revolutionized my life. I hope we are sharing the same experience!

8

No-Knock Policy

"What's wrong with me?" This was the heartrending question a little boy at camp asked his counselor after he had been totally rejected by his peers. "Why is it that my parents send me off to one camp after another? Why is it when I leave my duffle bag in the cabin, I come back and find my gear thrown all over the place? Why is it nobody wants to choose me to play on their team?"

The same question could have been asked by the "ugly" (by the world's standards) high school girl who, as a joke, had been selected on a write-in basis as the homecoming beauty queen. Her heartless schoolmates then primed the student body to stand up and give her a loud Bronx cheer when the mid-field presentation came. That girl will never be the same.

Most of us are deeply affected by what our parents, other authority figures in our lives, or our peers think of us. If we are deeply rejected by any of these—if they "knock" us or deprive us of love—our self-esteem suffers.

I heard in the late 1970s a beautiful talk on the

importance of self-love by Dan Webster, a sensitive minister to high school youth at Garden Grove Community Church in Orange County, California. He cited shocking statistics: Half of the high schoolers in his group came from broken homes. That's not surprising since divorces at that time exceeded marriages in Orange County. Half of the teenagers were on some kind of drugs—including animal tranquilizers, marijuana, and alcohol. The statistics on abortions, babies born out of wedlock, and venereal disease—even among the eleven- to thirteen-year-olds—were staggering.

Why these awesome statistics? According to Webster, the reason was lack of self-love in the young people he saw. Even the prettiest and handsomest couldn't imagine that a person they wanted to go out with would ever see anything in them to value. "Who are you kiddin'?" they would say. "He [or she] would *never* go out with me."

These feelings of inferiority are drummed into us at an early age and then often reinforced by our peers. Lack of acceptance, approval, and affection cause young people to withdraw or sometimes to join everything in sight in an effort to obtain popularity. And then they are willing to compromise—sexually, as well as other ways—just to get approval.

Dan Webster and his young people created a six-step program to increase self-love. They call it a "No-Knock Policy." I think these steps are equally applicable to all of us.

1. Realize the battle in your life between the voice of self-condemnation and the voice of self-affirmation. The negative voice can come from Satan or from the tapes recorded on our psyche long, long ago. The positive voice comes from God. As Dan puts it, "The Holy Spirit is our biggest cheerleader."

2. Let go of the chains of humiliation and rejection. Stop carrying them around. Trust God to heal the wounds. These negative traits we see in ourselves are really distortions of reality. They are seen through childish eyes.

3. Come to the point where you really believe what God says about you. You might be amazed to find in the Bible the great value God places on each one of us. He pronounced his creation "good"—even "very good."

4. Reflect in your moral decisions what God says about you. When we do what God expects of us, we end up feeling good about ourselves. If we act courageously, we feel good, not bad—the same when we forgive or show compassion, when we exhibit self-control or deeply care for and encourage others. Helping others is the greatest uplift in the world; it builds our feelings of self-worth and self-love.

5. Commit yourself to a life of significance. We are somebodies when we do something with

our lives. Mediocrity makes us sick. And the *most* important and significant thing we can do is care for God and others.

6. Commit yourself to a community of people who are working out the first five steps. The Christian life was not designed to be lived alone. You need the love, support, and affirmation of others to help you feel really good about yourself.

9

Family
Communication

I remember reading an article in *Denver* magazine describing the help available in that city for people in crisis. The writer made the significant comment that the basic miracle in family counseling is getting people to talk. Nearly every family specialist in Denver mentioned in the article said that noncommunication is the number one root of every family problem.

One hysterical mother couldn't get along with her four teenage sons. She couldn't talk to them, so she was on the verge of blowing herself and her children up by turning on the gas. A big brother purposefully broke his younger sister's arm. She could yell at her brother but couldn't really get through to him. A teenage son had terrible rows with his father. They could condemn each other but could not communicate.

One of the psychiatrists interviewed in the article commented that intimacy scares many people. When they experience intimacy in treatment, it's like a miracle; they learn to be close without being afraid. He cited an example of a teenage girl and her mother who had experienced a lack of communication for years. It was as if there were something wrong with having feelings in their family.

When the girl learned that her mother was suffering terminal cancer, she attempted suicide. She was actually angry that her mother was dying because she had never been able to talk to her. Then suddenly the situation became so traumatic they were finally able to start talking. The much-delayed communication enabled them to heal their relationship before the mother's death.

The counselors interviewed agreed that the first thing that has to happen in a marriage or family in trouble is the people involved must understand more of what their expectations are for themselves and one another. People have a lot of misconceptions. For example, men think they should know at birth what a woman enjoys and that no "real man" ever has to be told. Women believe that too. Another absurd expectation is, "If you loved me, you'd know what I want. Since you don't know, you don't even love me." In such a case, the mate's only recourse is to be psychic.

A social worker counseled her clients, "You keep saying 'he' this or 'she' that. How about 'I feel' or 'I want'? Talk to each other." A team leader said: "It helps if you can get past the defenses enough to share. . . . The only way to see miraculous change is for the family to admit change is needed, then work like hell."

All the experts seem to agree. The best (maybe only) way to work at family problems is to communicate. That may sound easy, but anyone who has tried it knows it is not. It's hard to reveal ourselves and let another human being see our weakness—see us as we really are with all the defense mechanisms down.

Maybe we don't even know ourselves as we really are. If we don't, let's not delay any longer in trying to find out. I think the best way we can learn who we are is to see ourselves through another's eyes. And that can come only through open and honest communication—not just blaming and criticizing and yelling, but heart-to-heart dialogue in a spirit of love and understanding. It entails sharing our deepest feelings, letting them see the light of day. Let's dig them out and start communicating today. I think we'll be amazed how it can help.

10

Don't Judge Yourself

An article in a Christian magazine carried a make-believe dialogue between a personified "Judgment" and a human being. In this dialogue, the letter *J* stood for Judgment and *M* for Man. I think the *J* could just as easily have stood for Jesus Christ and the *M* for me.

J said one very wise thing that I have also discovered for myself: "As you are easier on yourself, I see you less judgmental of others."

I have always been my own worst critic, and that simply means most of the time I'm excessively hard on myself. And at the same time, I've been critical of others, much more so than I should have been. I've begun to look at myself in a much more realistic light. I still see the sin and weakness in my life—some caused by my own willfulness and some the result of early childhood conditioning. But William Glasser in his *Reality Therapy*[7] insists the way to health is to accept things as they are (for the moment) and then get on with making responsible decisions that will enrich the rest of our lives.

Paul Tournier in *Escape from Loneliness* says, "The really important thing in life is not the avoidance of mistakes but the obedience of faith. By obedience the man is led step by step to correct his errors, whereas nothing will happen to him if he doesn't get going."[8]

For me, at least, there are two significant attitudes each of us must have: an acceptance of ourselves as we are without blaming others and a dissatisfaction with mediocrity. We must never be satisfied with anything but God's best. We do this as we come to love and accept ourselves, and begin to understand that God's best points toward the love and acceptance of others in a completely nonjudgmental way.

11

Dying to Self

C. S. Lewis, shortly after he became a Christian, wrote a good friend of his and stated that since he had begun to pray, he had gained a new self-concept. He realized his true worth as a person, that this was quite the opposite of self-involvement. As he put it, "You don't teach a seed how to die into treehood by throwing it into the fire; and it has to become a good seed before it's worth burying."[9]

Lewis is saying the self that is to die in response to Christ's call is (or should be) something really worthwhile, of real value. Christ wants to use a self that is vibrant and alive. The only thing that really dies is selfish ambition and pride. The real self is alive with the Spirit of God and willing to have God's will, instead of its own, be done.

Paul Tournier makes somewhat the same point in *A Place for You,*[10] in which he likens dying to self, so as to be reborn in Christ, to a trapeze artist in a circus. He or she must have a good firm grasp on the trapeze and be in motion before he or she can let go, fly through the air, and grasp the other swinging bar. Tournier adds, "It is very dangerous to let go of one's support if life is at a halt, whereas when life is in full swing one can easily let go of it in order to leap forward."

Tournier has observed that there are two significant but contrasting philosophies in the world. He calls them two gospels. The first of these, the gospel of psychology, urges us to assert and defend ourselves, to develop our abilities, to pursue our ambitions, to aggressively struggle for a place in life—in short, to discover ourselves and live life to the fullest. In contrast, the gospel of religion is a plea for self-denial, generosity, meekness, and love. It is a call to leave our places of security, to detach ourselves from selfish ambitions, and to give ourselves to the service of others. Some theologians preach this second gospel to their congregations; psychologists instill the first gospel in their counselees; and disciples of the two contrasting viewpoints line up in opposition to each other. (Thoughts for this paragraph were gleaned from *The Christian Psychology of Paul Tournier* by Gary Collins.[11])

According to Tournier, such opposition of psychology and religion is unnecessary. He again uses the trapeze analogy as an illustration. A person must first find a place in life and accept her- or himself as she or he *is* before moving on to loving service for others. These two contrasting ideologies—to assert oneself and then to deny self—are not mutually exclusive. They are complementary, Tournier feels. Lewis seems to feel the same way. Both men are in opposition to the "miserable worm" theology taught by some churches. Quite the contrary, the more we are fulfilled and vital and living the abundant life, the easier it is to die to selfish ambitions and follow the One who brought the abundant life in the first place. We *do* have to, as Lewis puts it, become a good seed before we are worth burying.

It is enormously important that we do not degrade ourselves. Christ doesn't want us to be miserable worms in order to follow him. Rather, he wants us to come to him with a feeling of joy and self-worth. This will happen as we die to the old selfish ways and are filled with God's grace and goodness and joy. Any seed planted by our Lord does grow into a healthy tree. It may have to be buried for a time while the roots are taking hold, but eventually it will sprout into something better than ever. Don't be afraid to die to self, for it is then that you experience your resurrection as you feel the thrill of letting go of the trapeze bar marked "self" and grasping firmly the new bar marked "life in Christ."

Encouraging Others

*Blessed be the God and Father of our
Lord Jesus Christ, the Father of mercies and the
God of all consolation, who consoles us in all
our affliction, so that we may be able to console
those who are in any affliction with the
consolation with which we ourselves are
consoled by God. For just as the sufferings of
Christ are abundant for us, so also our
consolation is abundant through Christ. If we
are being afflicted, it is for your consolation and
salvation; if we are being consoled, it is for your
consolation, which you experience when you
patiently endure the same sufferings that
we are also suffering.*

2 Corinthians 1:3-6 (NRSV)

12

Caring

I have discovered an exciting little book entitled *On Caring*[12] by Milton Meyerhoff. There is a wealth of wisdom crammed into about one hundred pages, but of primary importance to me is his definition of caring: wanting the other person to grow and helping him or her to do it. In further explanation, he writes:

> To care for another person, I must be able to understand him and his world as if I were inside it. I must be able to see, as it were, with his eyes what his world is like to him and how he *sees* himself. . . . I must go into his world in order to sense from the inside what life is like for him.
>
> In caring, my being *with* the other person is bound up with being *for* him as well: I am for him in his striving to grow and be himself. . . . In caring for another person I encourage him, I inspire him to have the courage to be himself. My trust in him encourages him to trust himself and to be worthy of the trust. Perhaps few things are more encouraging to another than to realize

that his growth evokes admiration, a sponta-
neous delight or joy, in the one who cares for
him. He experiences my admiration as assuring
him that he is not alone and that I am really for
him. I help him realize and appreciate what he
has done. It is as if I had said to him, "Look at
yourself now, see what you did, see what you
can do."

Before we can truly care for another, we must
understand that person. But we can only understand
another person if he or she opens up to us. In order to do
this, the person must have confidence that our relationship is completely free from any kind of judgment.

I remember an episode on a television show, in
which one of the characters, a company psychologist
and personal friend of another employee, told his friend
to open up about a problem. He said that he was there
to listen and not sit in judgment. The problem-ridden
person took him at his word and did just that. When the
friend-psychologist heard just how bad this man was
and what an atrocious thing he had done, he told him,
"You're disgusting. That's the most disgusting thing
I've ever heard. I don't ever want to have anything to
do with you again." And he walked away from him.

Although this was intended as a humorous episode
in the show, it wouldn't be so funny in our day-to-day
relationships. How different it all might be if we tried to
understand why other persons are the way they are, why
they act as they do, why they respond to certain stimuli

in a prescribed way. If we would only try to, as Meyer-hoff puts it, "see with his eyes what his world is like to him, and go into his world in order to sense from inside what life is like for him."

Really, isn't that what Christ did? Didn't he take on human form to be able to feel the way we do and experience the same kind of temptations that plague us?

In our relationships as lovers and relatives and friends, it is important that we try to get inside other persons and see what they see, experience what they feel. That doesn't mean we have to react in just the same way, but it is possible that frequently we'd react the same way if we were walking in their shoes.

Life becomes exciting and full of zest when we care enough to encourage and build up our friends and loved ones. Caring is love in action. It is God at work in our lives.

13

An Invitation
to Live

Sidney Jourard, in his book *The Transparent Self*, talks about an "invitation to die" that is given to people who commit suicide or seriously consider it. He says:

He [a person] will continue to live as long as he has hope of fulfilling meanings and values. As soon as meaning, value and hope vanish from a person's experience, he begins to stop living; he begins to die.

Now I am going to propose that *people destroy themselves in response to an invitation originating from others to stop living;* and that people *live* in response to the experience of invitations to continue living in some way, or in any possible way. . . .

Now one person can invite another to change his being in many ways. . . . When your purposes have worn out, when it seems that there is no place for you and your way of being a person in a given time and place, and when you feel you have already been abandoned by others, I can invite you to reinvent yourself and find challenge in new projects.[13]

There isn't much I can add to what Jourard has said except to ask a few questions. Have you ever "invited" anybody to die? Have you ever extended an "invitation" to anybody to *live*? Have you ever invited anyone to "find challenge in new projects"?

This subject is close to my heart. I was once invited to die by someone very close to me, not by an open expression but by the "indifference to the continued existence of the person" Jourard writes about. I would have accepted the invitation had it not been for many counter-invitations to live, extended by so many who showed me love and the "challenge in new projects." The new project was Jesus Christ. Can you think of a better one? Can you think of a better "hope of fulfilling meaning"? I can't.

I write this chapter with great fear and trepidation. The last thing I want to do is lay a guilt trip on family members or friends who survive a suicide victim. A main thrust of this book is to encourage you to get rid of guilt complexes and start feeling positive about yourself.

Many times there is absolutely nothing we can do to prevent such a tragic taking of life. Sometimes the person who takes his or her life has reached such a level of despondency there is little or nothing anyone can do about it. The causes may be emotional or merely physical. A tremendous loss can drive almost anyone to deep despair. A psychologist once told me I wouldn't be normal if I were not depressed over certain circumstances in my life. How many of us can honestly say we have never considered suicide? Or wished that we were dead? I used to call frequently on older perons in retirement homes, many of whom told me they prayed daily God would take them.

My sympathy and empathy go out to survivors of a suicide of a loved one and to those who are contemplating such an act. Not to mention those who have left us. I read once a definition of the suicidal mindset that I agree with: It isn't that the person wants to die; it's just that the pain of living is too much. I sit in judgment on no man or woman who takes his or her own life, or wants to. I no longer feel that way myself, but I am in no position to cast the first stone at anyone!

Before this day is over, will you extend an invitation to live to another, especially someone in your own family? Will you love that person and invite him or her to a new life in Jesus Christ?

14

The Seeds of Love

George Vaillant in *Adaptation to Life*[14] makes a profound statement: "The seeds of love must be eternally resown. . . . My guess is that we stop growing when our human losses are no longer replaced. Without love it is hard to grow."

Carl Rogers, in a speech made in 1964, said:

When I am not prized, or not appreciated, I not only feel very much diminished, I *am* greatly diminished in my behavior. When I am prized, I blossom. I expand, I am an interesting individual. In a group which is hostile or unappreciative I am just not much of anything. People wonder with very good reason, how did he ever get a reputation? I wish I had the strength to be somewhat more similar in both kinds of groups, but actually the person I am in a warm and interested group is very different from the person I am in a hostile or a cold group.[15]

Love freely given and love freely received are major

ingredients in any whole and growing life. Affirmation brings out the best in people. Hostility and lack of appreciation stifle and squelch the human spirit. Knowing this, how do we relate to those around us? Are we sowing the seeds of love?

15

Altruism

In the last chapter I mentioned *Adaptation to Life*[16] by George Vaillant. The book is a detailed report of a thirty-year study of a number of men who, in their college days, were deemed logical candidates for success. Many did succeed. Many failed. The study attempted to find out why.

Several comments by the author particularly interested me: "The gratified child can postpone gratification, and adults only act 'spoiled' if they have received too little love—not too much. . . . Until someone has something for which to be genuinely grateful, altruism proves too difficult a psychological balancing act." Altruism is defined as "getting pleasure from giving to others what you yourself would like to receive."

Vaillant has discovered a great Christian truth: Altruism is too difficult without having something to be genuinely grateful for. We cannot reach out in unselfish love to others until we have experienced the love of Christ in our own lives.

In my times of deep depression, before I felt the

redeeming love of Christ, I was not genuinely grateful. I
was told by others to "do something for somebody else
and you'll feel better yourself." I *couldn't*. Vaillant says
it would have been "too difficult a psychological balancing act."

A biblical example of this is the story of Peter in
John 21. Peter was so depressed over his denial of
Christ that even Jesus' resurrection brought him no joy.
His guilt was weighting him down. He couldn't fulfill
his mission of being the holder of the keys of the kingdom. He couldn't do the works of altruism and compassion he had been commanded to do.

However, when Jesus came to Peter reassuring him
of his continuing love, Peter did feel genuinely grateful.
He was empowered to feed Jesus' flock. There is no
gratitude like the gratitude felt by a redeemed and forgiven person—a person given another chance when he
or she has blown all previous ones.

There are two things that will help us set others
free to do works of altruism. We can love and we can
forgive. The love takes away the spoiledness and self-
centeredness that come from not being loved. And
the forgiveness will make them genuinely grateful—
grateful enough to reach out to others in love and
compassion.

We hold the keys to the kingdom of altruism in the
lives of the significant others in our families and in the
world. We can use those keys to open up lives to altruism or to imprison them in a dungeon of unforgiveness
and lack of love. The choice is ours!

16

A Key to
Mental Health

I have a feeling that a real clue to a man's mental health and stability is found in the relationship he has with his father. If he can feel genuine love and warmth for his father and be able to express it, then I think he is in a position different from that of the man who feels no love for his dad or can't express it.

I remember reading a testimonial given by a young pastor at the memorial service for his father. It was called "A Son Remembers His Father," and ends:

> You remember him as a pastor and a friend, my mother remembers him as a loving husband, Paul and I remember him as our father who was without a doubt the kindest, most loving man we have ever known—a man to whom I was able to say on the last day I saw him before his death—and these were my last words to him—"I love you, Dad." It was easy for us to say that, for Dad was an easy man to love!

I think it works both ways. I think fathers need to be

able to say to their sons, "I love you." I remember John Powell's account of his father's death. Powell was weeping, and when a nurse in the hospital tried to console him, he told her, "I'm not weeping because my father died [the man was in great pain and death was a release]. I'm crying because he never told me he loved me." Apparently his father did love him. The mother reassured the son on that point. But the father had never *said* so.

If you're a son, think through your relationship with your father. Do you love him? Have you told him so?

If you're a dad, when was the last time you told your son you loved him? You'll note that I said "*told*" him. You can't get off the hook by saying, "He knows. I buy him groceries, don't I?" or "I bought him a new pair of blue jeans last week."

I believe the greatest healing agent in life is love—and the ability to express it. Here is the key for real mental health and stability. The Christian gospel commands us to love one another, but of equal importance is the ability to say to another person, "I love you . . . I need you."

17

Make My
Garden Grow

I am indebted to one of my newest Christian friends for most of the thoughts expressed in the rest of this chapter. I want to quote her from a personal letter.

As gardens we so often need others to care for us and help us grow. Under one person's care, we flourish. Under another's, we wilt and die a bit (or a lot). I am grateful with you that you have found some loving gardeners in the last few years.

So much of what you said, I feel too. How important it is to help others untangle conflicts, guilt and anger; how others often underestimate the difficulty of overcoming depression; how the best thing one can do is to go with them, step-by-step; how feelings must be shared to be dealt with; how the Christian life is not all victory and roses.

As you said, only love can help one think well of oneself, and unless a person thinks some good of himself, he cannot improve. A paradox of which I've read more than once: Accept me as I am and I can change.

Former television newscaster Walter Cronkite once spoke of a high school teacher he had back in Texas. The man affirmed young Walter and gave him the impetus and courage needed to forge a brilliant career in the news media. Cronkite said, "A vote of confidence can be inspiring stuff."

I remember watching a television movie based on the life of Little Mo Connolly, the famed tennis star who reached the heights of her career at an early age, then met with a tragic accident and death by cancer at thirty-four. I was struck by a bit of conversation between Mo's mother, a woman with little self-confidence, and her aunt. The aunt said, "If I could buy you for the price you set on yourself, and sell you for the price you're worth, I'd be the wealthiest woman in California."

The price we set on ourselves is far too often the price established by unworthy gardeners. We all need gardeners who will care for us and help us grow. We need those votes of confidence—what inspiring stuff!

18

Affirming Gifts

I had a letter from a friend who said, "To have one's gifts *received* well is just as important as giving them." She was talking about spiritual gifts, but the thought struck me that the same principle would apply to the giving and receiving of any kind of gift. Who wants to give a Christmas or birthday present to a wife or husband or friend and have them turn up their noses at it?

Later I read *Journey Inward—Journey Outward* [17] by Elizabeth O'Connor in which she also refers to the importance of giving and receiving gifts.

> One of the first steps in loving another is to let God call into being our own unique charisma: Love is an event in which we give ourselves to another. . . .
>
> If our own potential is blocked and has found no creative channels in which to flow, then what we feel in the presence of another is envy. We may not recognize it as envy—only a perplexing pain or deadness. We will have no praise of another—no joy in another. Instead, we will turn

away and in subtle ways seek to destroy the other. This is why we cannot get on with the business of loving unless we are discovering our own gift.

We need to discover and exercise our own gifts if we are to be a celebrating people, open to life. We need to be shepherds and cross that invisible line where the emphasis of our lives is more on giving than receiving.

That isn't to say we won't need to continue receiving the gifts of others. Life is a continuum of both receiving and giving; we cannot make it on our own without the spiritual gifts of others. That is the way the Christian life is designed. Our task is not only to exercise our own gifts but to call forth and affirm the gifts of others.

Of all the worthwhile and challenging things Elizabeth O'Connor says in her book, the most exciting to me is the hope of belonging to a community "whose task was not only the exercising of its own gifts, but calling forth the gifts of others." The best way we can do that is to affirm those gifts.

19

Warts and All

Loving people "warts and all" means we really love them with all their faults and failings. I'm a great advocate of "warts-and-all" love, of unconditional love.

But that's a lot easier said than done. Unfortunately, while I'm an advocate of unconditional love, I'm not very good at it. Someone's warts can turn me off. It's a lot easier to love the lovable than the unlovable.

C. S. Lewis, in *The Voyage of the Dawn Treader,*[18] has a marvelous insight into this warts-and-all business. Lucy has found a spell which allows her to see and hear what her friends are saying about her. She can actually see them and hear their words, even though they are in England and she is in the land of Narnia. While eavesdropping on some friends, she hears one say of her: "Not a bad little kid in her way. But I was getting pretty tired of her before the end of term." Lucy's immediate (and natural) response is: "Well, you jolly well won't have the chance any other term. Two-faced little beast."

But what Lucy doesn't know is that this girl really does like her. It's just that she is in the company of an older girl whom she is unsure of, and so she's afraid to speak out in favor of her friend Lucy. It was easier to respond critically and not risk losing the companionship of the girl who had accused her of being all "taken up" with Lucy. Lucy doesn't understand this and puts the worst possible interpretation on her friend's remark. This is another natural (and paranoiac) response.

Then Aslan, the Christ figure in the story, does a great thing for Lucy. He helps her to see her friends as they really are and to accept them in their weakness—warts and all. Lewis' teaching is that nobody loves us purely (nor we anybody else). We all have human qualities. We're weak and we vacillate. God's grace is to help us accept even faulty human love and not misjudge it. It's God's will for us to have a genuine relationship with people within our frailty and within their frailty, and then to have that relationship covered by his grace.

I once read an article about Bud Grant, who was a highly successful coach of the Minnesota Vikings professional football team. It was the author's opinion that Grant succeeded because he combined "intensity with common decency." This coach controlled what he could control, and accepted what he couldn't. Some coaches fail because they're unable to do this. The author tells the story of a Vikings wide receiver who couldn't run some difficult inside patterns. Grant accepted this and used the player's strengths instead. That player helped win many games for the team.

Apparently Bud Grant accepted the "warts" of his players, saw their good points, and used them. He didn't try to force players into his ideas of what they should be, pushing them into failure.

Nothing can be as consuming as failure. How about those you love? Can you love them in spite of their failures, their shortcomings, their warts? Can you see, as C. S. Lewis did so clearly, that no love is pure, that we all have to love others in the midst of our frailty and theirs? Do we not expect too much from them? Can we accept their love and friendship as coming from an imperfect human being and, therefore, not pure? If we can, if we can be a realist like a C. S. Lewis or a Bud Grant, we'll have much more peace. But if we demand more from others (and ourselves) than we can reasonably expect, we're going to end up being consumed by failure, both theirs and ours.

I came across this graphic admonition to look out for our own warts:

> If you suddenly gained the muscle power of a hundred men and could outwrestle King Kong, it doesn't mean you still wouldn't have to worry about dandruff, or acne, or hemorrhoids, right?

Right!

20

Support

A lecturer I once heard discussed the basic needs of people. He explained the ideas and theories of several famous psychiatrists and psychologists, including Freud, Adler, Jung, and Frank. The consensus was that our three most important needs are to be loved, to feel important, and to feel secure. Anyone who relates to us in a way whereby we feel this way about ourselves is supportive in a very positive way.

It seems to me that giving support to others and receiving support from others is a little bit of what life is all about. I like Paul Tournier's comment in his magnificent book entitled *A Place for You*:[19]

> I, too, quote writers and scientists in order to lean on them and on their authority, which I enhance by the very fact of quoting them. We lean on each other for support in our fight for the same cause.

How wonderful it is to be able to lean on each other for support!

One day I was feeling discouraged over a personal situation. Then I had lunch with a bright young minister friend whom I'd come to respect highly. This young man went out of his way to express appreciation for my ideas and my writing. I learned that he was working on a sermon and was interested in incorporating certain of my thoughts and feelings into it. His genuine interest in me set my spirits soaring. I came away from our luncheon feeling much less discouraged and with a renewed dedication to keep on going, to speak out even more boldly for Christ, to express my opinions, to keep on writing, to reach out to help others in the valley of discouragement.

This was what his support did for me, and that set me thinking. If the lecturer is correct in his assumption that all of us need to feel important and to feel worthwhile—and I believe he is—then how much good can we do for those we know and love by supporting them, by telling them how important they are and how much they mean to us?

During that lecture the wife of my closest friend leaned over and said, "We love you." She had no way of knowing just how much I needed that affirmation—how much I needed to know at that moment that someone really cared for me.

As I have reflected on my own feelings and needs, I see now how important it is, not to destroy others by our nagging and our criticisms and our withholding of a pat on the back. Instead we need to look for good in them. With God's help we need to daily practice the art of affirming and supporting, of being able to openly express love and confidence. And we can then begin to see life-changing miracles working in their lives and ours.

21

Acceptance

I could write a thousand books on acceptance and still not begin to cover the subject. I could write about what *kind* of acceptance, acceptance of whom, by whom, of what, and all the ramifications thereof. I could write about conditional acceptance and nonconditional acceptance. All would stress the vital importance of being accepted, whether we're talking about being accepted by others, or accepting others, or—perhaps most important of all—accepting ourselves. But I'd like to examine here just one aspect of acceptance, i.e., how we can be one person with someone who accepts us as we are unconditionally, and an entirely different person with someone who doesn't accept us, or rejects us, or with a total stranger who doesn't know us at all.

I noticed this phenomenon firsthand when I was in New York and called an old friend I hadn't seen in six years. I went out to his house to spend the night with his family, and it was just like old times. Our friendship picked up right where we'd left it six years before. We still had the same interests, and we were still the same people. And while my Christian faith has become the most important dimension in my life—not the case the last time we were together or in the early years of our friendship—that didn't prevent us from sharing the same camaraderie we have had for many years.

I am one person to these particular friends. They know me well. If someone asked them to tell all about Bill Kinnaird, I feel they would be able to give a very accurate answer. And I think I am that particular person with them because they accept me. They know my failings and foibles as well as anybody else. I've never tried to hide my humanity from them. But that doesn't bother them. Their friendship and unconditional acceptance bring out the very best in me. I'm relaxed with them, not on the defensive, not trying to prove anything, not feeling any need to justify myself. And, in a very real sense, I like the person they see in me.

On the other hand, some people seem to bring out the worst in me. I react poorly when I'm around them because they are critical of me, and I don't respond favorably to criticism. I'm struggling with those negative reactions and asking the Lord to help me deal with them.

You see, I believe that when we become Christians there isn't an overnight change in our personalities, but there *is* a basic change at the center. Slowly but surely, power emanates from that center (which has become Christ) to clear up areas in our lives which may not be all that we or he would have them be. Christ's admonition to us to be perfect (Matthew 5:48) can easily be misunderstood, but to me this scripture means that we are to *strive* to be "perfect" and that he will help us through his Holy Spirit. To be sure, we will fall short and fail. We are not going to be perfect in this life. Anyone who has read and related to the last part of Romans 7, in which Paul says that he still does the things he doesn't want to do and doesn't do the things he should, will understand. All of us fail. All of us are less than perfect. But as Paul also says in Romans 8, there's a way out. There's someone who will help us in our efforts to strive for perfection and to be more Christlike, and that someone is Christ himself. When we fall down, as we inevitably will do, he will pick us up, dust us off, and send us on our way again, with his Holy Spirit as our constant companion or comforter.

When I have friends who will forgive me my failings, who will give me that much-needed word of encouragement, who will hang in there with me regardless, then I'm more like the person I feel I truly am, the person God intends me to be. But when I run across someone who won't forgive me, who knocks me down instead of picking me up, who criticizes rather than encourages, I have an all-too-human tendency to lash back, to justify myself. Then I'm *not* being the person God intends me to be or the person I truly am.

My point of emphasis here is the importance of helping others—and especially the members of one's own family—to become the people they truly are down deep, the people God intends them to be. How can we accomplish this? Accept them, love them, encourage them, and give them a most precious gift: freedom to fail. There is no greater liberation from bondage than the feeling that we can fail, we can be less than perfect, we can make mistakes—and still be loved and accepted.

22

We Need Each Other

One day at the office I was talking to an associate about his particular area of expertise, one in which I have absolutely no capabilities. I told him so. I said, "If I had to do your job, our company would be in terrible shape." His reply, a very kind and considerate one, was: "I couldn't do your job, either. The company needs both of us."

Without saying so, he had stumbled upon one of the basic tenets of the Christian faith—one too frequently overlooked in many circles. It's phrased most aptly in 1 Corinthians 12. In this chapter, Paul is talking about the special, but different, spiritual gifts each of us has and how these gifts should work together for the benefit of the body of Christ. He lists a number of these gifts, and then goes on to say that, just as in a human body the foot is no more important than the hand and the eye is no more important than an ear, there shouldn't be a priority of spiritual gifts. They are all needed if the body is to function the way God intends.

Ray Stedman has written an excellent book in this

area called *Body Life,*[20] in which he points out how crucial it is that the body of Christ come together to help one another. Just as the man at the office and I have different capabilities—I couldn't do his job, and he possibly couldn't do mine, but we work together for the benefit of the same management—we Christians should work together for the benefit of our "Management" and for one another.

Unfortunately, though, we don't work together when we wrangle and argue over doctrine, or who is the most important in the kingdom, or whether another's spiritual experience is valid. Suppose the man at the office and I got into an argument over some minor (or even major) policy matter or I thought I was more important than he or that his job wasn't as important as mine. How much productive work would we get done? How much would we help each other and our fellow employees?

Ron Davis, a pastor and a good friend of mine, once preached a sermon on the body coming together to help one another with their spiritual gifts. In it he told a true story of a lady who had been given up as a hopeless case by a psychiatrist. She was in a deep depression, and the professionals said she would get no better. However, she started attending a small group at her church, and the unconditional love and affirmation of those in the group nursed her back to health in a matter of months. She was able to go on and lead a fulfilling life. Nobody had told the group she was an impossible case, and if they had been told that, I suspect they would have replied, "We are dealing with a God to whom *all* things are possible."

Davis went on to say: "It's my conviction that in many spirit-filled churches this [healing by love and affirmation] is becoming more and more . . . commonplace, as Christians begin to understand that they have been given a beautiful, mysterious power by the Lord, . . . and as they allow the Holy Spirit to work in them as plain ordinary Christians [lay persons]."

His whole point is that the Church, the body of Christ, is made up of people with spiritual gifts and that if we love one another, we can use these gifts for the benefit of the whole. We can say to one hurting and in trouble: "With the Holy Spirit as my strengthener, I will give you my whole self, my whole life. I'm not going to rest until you become all God wants you to be, until you become a whole person in Jesus Christ."

That's what spiritual gifts are for. That's what people are for. That's what our brothers and sisters in Christ are for. Our Management needs our gifts. And the world needs them too.

23

Hand in Hand

While watching a televised episode of "Little House on the Prairie," I thought of the quotation from Isaiah: "And a little child shall lead them." The child Laura was leading a blind man through the woods and mountains trying to find the way back to Morgan's Creek, where they could get a doctor to tend her badly wounded father. The man hadn't strayed far from his lonely cabin for years because he was afraid—afraid of stumbling, afraid of losing his way. He had very reluctantly accompanied Laura on this journey because he was the only one who knew how to find Morgan's Creek. They hoped for success with the blind man's memory and Laura's eyes.

However, the blind man's memory started to fail, and in a very poignant scene he broke down and cried out, "Child, I'm afraid." Laura's reassuring reply was, "Then we'll be afraid together."

That's it! That's the key. Not being unafraid, but being afraid together. Paul Tournier in *The Strong and the Weak* says: "The Christian is not exempt from fear, but he takes his fears to God. Faith does not suppress fear; what it does is allow one to go forward in spite of it."[21]

But how much better if we have someone's hand to hold onto as we both take our mutual fears to God. How much better if we don't have to go it alone. And how much better if we can express our fear to someone else instead of keeping it bottled up inside.

The blind man and Laura, after their shared expression of fear, were able to find Morgan's Creek and take help to Laura's father. They almost didn't make it; they lost their way several times and almost gave up. First it was the blind man who was discouraged and needed reassurance. Then later Laura became discouraged and almost gave up. When this happened the blind man repeated verbatim the very words she had used in encouraging him to keep going when he desperately wanted to quit. Each needed to know that he or she wasn't the only one afraid, that the other was also afraid, but was going on.

In his book *To Understand Each Other*, Paul Tournier gives us some interesting insights into our need to share feelings and words with another person:

> How beautiful, how grand and liberating this experience is, when couples learn so to help each other. It is impossible to overemphasize the immense need men have to be really listened to, to be taken seriously, to be understood. . . . No one can develop freely in this world and find a

full life without feeling understood by at least one person. . . . He who would see himself clearly must open up to a confidant freely chosen and worthy of such trust. It may be a friend just as easily as a doctor; it may also be one's marital partner.[22]

It was in the dialogue of free expression that Laura and the blind man were able to reassure and help each other and thus keep going. The result was the blind man's renouncing his cowardice of ten years and saying: "That kind of guilt [cowardice] is a far sight worse than dyin'. . . . We're gonna keep on walkin' till we find it."

Find it they did, but only because they had each other to open up to, to express their fear to, and to hold hands with. And it is here that we find help through all the fears of life, as we take them to God in confidence that he will help us, and as we find someone we can open up to and be completely honest with about our feelings. Then, if we can find somebody to hold hands with, we can move out confidently toward the Morgan's Creek in our lives and keep on walking until we find it.

24

If I Were You

Have you ever been involved with an "if I were you I'd . . ." person? I have. During the time when I was greatly depressed and barely able to function, a Christian leader in the community told me (in rather harsh tones), "Why don't you pray to God to change your attitude!" Another person, never having come close to experiencing the things I had, said, "If it were me, I'd like to think I would have reacted differently."

By contrast, a warm, loving pastor friend of mine said, "If that had happened to me, I don't know what I'd have done. I'd have probably ended up in a padded room to keep me from knocking my brains out."

Who was the most helpful and comforting? Was it the one who chastised me, or the one who loved me, empathized with me, and didn't hold me up to ridicule and scorn, who said that if he had been in my shoes, he might have felt the same way or worse?

Picture with me the scene in the twenty-first chapter of John. Peter is probably experiencing great depression, even after the resurrection of Christ. His beloved

Jesus has achieved the victory he had said he would, but Peter realizes his own weakness. He is fully aware that he has denied the Master. The other apostles cluster around Peter. Do they say, "Why don't you pray to God to change your attitude?" No. Do they say, "Jesus gave you the keys to the kingdom. Why don't you get off your duff and go preach the Good News?" No, they don't say that either. What do they say? "We'll go fishing *with* you." They hang in there with their friend.

Nothing is more unattractive, more unappealing, less helpful than an "if I were you I would" person. And nothing is more helpful than an "if I were in your shoes I don't know what I'd do" person—one who will say, "I'll hang in there with you."

25

Special Glue

There can be many meaningful friendships outside the bonds of Christianity. I myself have friends who are not Christians and yet who mean very much to me. But there is a special glue holding Christian friendships together.

One of my minister friends taught a course called "The 3:00 A.M. Christian." He was trying to teach us how to be the kind of friend someone in trouble wouldn't hesitate to awaken in the middle of the night. I'd feel free to call some of my Christian friends at any hour of the day or night.

I once called some Christian friends who live in a distant city and whom I hadn't talked to or heard from in a long time. We picked right up where we had left off. We had the mutual bond of Christ and could share our experiences and relate what our Lord has been doing in our lives. One lady has been praying for a particular need of mine for over five years, and she assured me she is still praying about it. No matter how far apart in miles, we are never apart in spirit.

I have a friend in London with whom I am bonded by that special glue of Christian friendship. Our backgrounds are dissimilar, but we have in common the most important thing in the world—Jesus Christ. During a very difficult period in my life, she gave me unconditional, warm, Christian love. Do you think five thousand miles (or a million miles) could ever separate us? We care about each other—genuinely care. But had we not been Christians and open to being used in whatever way the Lord wanted to use us, our paths would never have crossed. Now I'm sure we will spend eternity still loving and caring for each other.

Undoubtedly each of us has those special persons in his or her life who give lavishly of themselves to us and to whom we can give ourselves without reservation. Relationships bonded with the glue of Christian love and commitment are special miracles that seem to come from the hand of God.

Now and then, as we find ourselves on the day-to-day treadmill of life, there may be times when it seems we become "unglued." Fractured relationships mar our lives, and the joy and peace and presence of the Lord seem remote within ourselves. We feel alone and alienated and out of step. In those moments, though, we can know beyond a doubt that the glue of the Holy Spirit can and will bond the pieces together again and restore broken feelings and broken relationships. God understands our hurts and needs and is eager for us to live whole, joyful, productive lives in relationship with others.

26

Friendship

One of my favorite authors is C. S. Lewis. Some of his observations make me say, "That's right; that's so right," and I want to share them with my friends.

Such are some quotes from his book *The Four Loves*.[23] The chapter on "Friendship" is particularly appealing to me. Lewis' sagacity is proven by his conclusions as to what friendship is.

In distinguishing friendship from *eros,* or "falling in love," Lewis says: "Lovers are normally face-to-face, absorbed in each other; friends, side by side, absorbed in some common interest." Friends are those who share something in common, whether it be collecting stamps, playing golf, or having a common bond in Jesus Christ and being excited about spiritual matters.

Friends are those who aren't using one another for some selfish purpose. Even the need to be needed can be symbiotic and sometimes neurotic. We all know, either firsthand or through fiction, of mothers who have a sick need to be needed. These are the more heinous types—the ones we've seen portrayed on the soap operas or in the movies—who try to keep their children dependent—upon them. True friends avoid that kind of clinging.

We come to know and love our friends by standing beside them in a common cause or when seeking after a mutual goal. This is especially true of Christian friends who have between them and among them the common bond of Jesus Christ. I think there are no deeper nor more committed friendships than those that include Christ. Since I have such friends, I can say that from my own experience. I know they are there to stand by me through thick and thin, no matter how tough the going, no matter how glaring my human weakness.

27

Priesthood of All Believers

The term "priesthood of all believers" is a more or less theological term that we see occasionally in Christian literature. What does it mean? I think it can mean a number of things, but technically I think the meaning is that all believers in and followers of Jesus Christ are "ministers" or "priests" to one another. We don't have to be ordained to minister. Leaving ministering to the exclusive province of the clergy is one of the greatest tragedies in the Christian church—a complete distortion of the teachings of Christ. We are responsible for ministering to one another's needs.

How can we minister to one another? Obviously, many ways. But I want to concentrate here on just one aspect of ministry: witnessing to the Gospel of Christ or conveying God's message to the world and to our Christian brothers and sisters.

Ray Stedman, in his book *Authentic Christianity,*[24] insists that the message of Christ is personally delivered by lay persons. He further believes that the function of the ordained minister is to equip us as lay persons to go out into the world and be messengers and servants of our Lord. He puts it this way:

> The good news does not come by means of angels. It is not announced from heaven by loud, impersonal voices. It doesn't even come by poring over dusty volumes from the past. In each generation it is delivered by living, breathing men and women who speak from their own experience. Most of us seem to require models which we can follow. Love must somehow become visible before it is caught by others. There is a strong personal element about the Gospel which cannot be eliminated without harm.

Dietrich Bonhoeffer makes the same point in his *Life Together,* a discussion of Christian fellowship and what it means to those partaking in it:

> God has put this Word [about Christ] into the mouth of men in order that it may be communicated to other men. When one person is struck by the Word, he speaks it to others. God has willed that we should seek and find his living Word in the witness of a brother. Therefore the Christian needs another Christian who speaks God's Word to him. He needs him again and again when he becomes uncertain and discouraged, for by himself he cannot help himself. He needs his brother man as a bearer and proclaimer of the divine Word.

> The Christ in our heart is weaker than the Christ in the word of his brother; his own heart is uncertain, his brother's is sure.[25]

How much we need others to give us encouragement in time of despair, and hope to go on when everything seems meaningless! And where does that hope and encouragement come from? It comes from the Word. It comes from finally realizing we are not alone, that we'll never be alone, neither now nor in the life to come. It comes from the dawning realization that the promises in scripture are true: there *is* a living Jesus Christ who will come to live in us and comfort us through his Holy Spirit. It comes when we realize our life revolves around him and in him and that he has gone to prepare an even greater place for us. This Word comes through the "priesthood of all believers."

28

Charity Begins
in the Home

The old saying "charity begins at home" can have both a positive and negative connotation. The selfish person can use it as an excuse and justification for not reaching out to others outside his "home" environment, however we define that term.

For some, unfortunately, home is limited to themselves. That's narcissism at its worst. I know one mother who told her son, "Keep your eye picked. The world's agin' you. If you don't think about yourself, nobody else will."

I know of a psychologist who told a wife and mother, "Stop thinking about your husband and children. Think about yourself." Such advice, if taken, would limit charity to an extremely narrow sphere—namely, me and my own self-interest.

There are others, though, who extend their charity a little further to their families. But the home is the home, and not much more than that. I've heard reports that some of the Mafia dons are most generous and kind as fathers. But when they go out the front door, they will shoot down anyone who stands in their path.

Then there are those who limit their charity to those *outside* the home. There are pillars of the church who are tyrants at home. There are those who are all for mission giving and taking care of the poor, but who hardly give their own children a second thought. Out of these families come many rebellious children who kick over the traces of the Christian faith because of the great hypocrisy they see in their homes.

There are also those, who while wanting to serve God and help others, seem to forget that those closest to them need help too. They seem to think it is easier, and perhaps safer, to help the anonymous than it is to aid those they know by name.

I am one who is motivated by a desire to help others. I have been helped so much myself that I deem it an obligation to reach out to others, and I have a great desire to do so. It brings joy and fulfillment; to me there is nothing more satisfying than helping.

Yet I think I may sometimes fall into the trap I'm writing about here. I'm afraid I see the ones I want to help as anonymous. Who are they, anyway, these people I want to help? As I write this, I'm considering some further training that would enable me to help people communicate better and thereby enrich their relationships. But I don't know personally yet any of these people I want to help.

I think one of the reasons we tend to reach out more to the anonymous than the known is that it is safer. We don't have to get as emotionally involved. The pain of rejection may not be as great. We aren't risking as much. To get deeply involved with someone we know can be a hazardous undertaking. Ministering to John or Jane Doe could be relatively easy, but ministering to my best friend or my son can be extremely difficult.

Let our ministry and our charity *begin* at home. I am not saying it should *end* there. And I am including in the home territory all whom we already know—not only our families, but our friends, our co-workers, our neighbors on the block.

Some of them may be in great need. There may be deep hurts we can help heal. Let's not limit our charity to the anonymous of this world. The Lord may be calling us to minister to those we know best. Maybe he has brought them into our lives for this very purpose.

God's Encouragement

*Indeed, we felt that we had received
the sentence of death so that we would
rely not on ourselves but on God
who raises the dead.*

2 Corinthians 1:9 (NRSV)

29

Your Own Moon

One morning on the "Good Morning, America" television show, host David Hartman interviewed Buzz Aldrin and Cliff Robertson. Aldrin is the astronaut who walked on the moon in 1969, and Robertson is the actor who portrayed him in the TV movie *Return to Earth.*

After his return from the moon walk to great fame and notoriety, Aldrin had a severe mental breakdown, accompanied by deep depression and a bout with alcoholism. At the time of the interview, he was on the road back, but like all of us he still had a way to go. When Hartman asked him if he knew the reason for his breakdown and depression, Aldrin replied that his life had been made up of one series of goals after another, culminating in the great goal of walking on the moon. For years his life had been centered on that one goal. It was his all-consuming passion, and when it was all over, he experienced a shattering letdown. There was a great void in his life with nothing to fill it, and depression began to seep in until it took over and almost destroyed him. He experimented with a number of things like alcohol and another woman (even though he was married) to try to deaden the pain. These seemed to give him temporary relief, but underneath it all his life was oppressed with a crippling lack of purpose.

At this point in the interview, Robertson entered into the conversation and stated that he could empathize with Aldrin. He said he thought we are all prone to depression if life is empty of meaning, if all our goals have been reached (or despaired of), and we are no longer gripped by an all-consuming passion that gives us the incentive to get out of bed eagerly every morning, looking forward with great anticipation to the events of the day.

That is true of me. At one point in my life, I too was plagued with great depression. My problem wasn't that my goals had all been met; they hadn't. But everything on which I had built my life came crumbling down around me. I had built my house on the sand that Christ talked about instead of solid rock, and when the strong winds of life beat against my house, it wasn't strong enough to stand up under the onslaught. Neither was Buzz Aldrin's. And even the successful Cliff Robertson, an Academy Award winner and a fine actor, could relate and empathize, could realize that we are all subject to depression given the right set of circumstances.

How important it is for each of us to be able to empathize with those who are being tried by the fire of depression. After all, until we have passed through a similar fire—the loss of a child or a mate or a career or whatever—we can't anticipate our own reactions.

Depression can rock anyone—even individuals who appear successful. For example, Winston Churchill, one of the most revered (and sometimes criticized) men in twentieth century history, was subject to terrible struggles with depression—the "Black Dog" he called it. So was Abraham Lincoln. With all the strain both these men were under in trying to save their own countries, it's no wonder. It would be extremely difficult to be optimistic with bombs bursting all over your cherished London, or with your native land torn apart at the seams, with brother fighting and killing brother.

I certainly don't have an easy answer to all depression, but I suspect some of it could be caused by chemical imbalance or deficiency. Situational depression, the kind I had, is horrible to confront when the situation doesn't change. But for me and hundreds of thousands of others, there is a way out of most depression. It is by having a reason for living, a goal—one that can never be totally fulfilled in this life because it's a growing and changing experience. There will always be something new and exciting—a new insight, a new understanding, new people to meet. There is the opportunity to help and be helped, to love and be loved. It is as we confront life with this attitude that we will discover change taking place in our lives, and we will come to see ourselves and others in a different light.

Whether we're Buzz Aldrin or Cliff Robertson or Winston Churchill or Abraham Lincoln—or simply Joe or Jane Citizen—we need a goal, a meaning in life, something to live for (and, if need be, die for). And it's ours for the asking in Jesus Christ. He will provide the meaning. He will *be* the meaning. How do I know? Because I have experienced it myself.

Buzz Aldrin said, "Everybody has his own moon." What's yours? Whatever it is, it need not destroy you. There's somebody who made the moon, and he holds you and me and all the "moons" in our lives in the palm of his hand.

30

Me Too, Dietrich

Dietrich Bonhoeffer was a great Christian martyr of the twentieth century, put to death by the Nazis for following the dictates of his faith and conscience in standing up to Hitler. At one point early in World War II, he was safely away from his native Germany, but chose to return home and risk the outcome. He felt that to be a Christian meant living out our faith and taking a stand for it, even if it meant loss of life.

How many of us would do that? Would I? I don't think any of us could answer without being in the situation. It's so easy to say what we would do, as opposed to what another person did. It's so easy to say we wouldn't break under torture, wouldn't divulge military secrets no matter what the enemy did to us. I remember as a child seeing a movie in which a prisoner of war broke under the torture of having bamboo sticks jammed under his nails and lit. His fellow prisoners disowned him for his cowardice. Yet, in the end, he turned out to be the greatest hero of all, saving the lives of his comrades by risking his own.

I can relate to Dietrich Bonhoeffer, not in his bravery or patriotism, but in his weakness. While in prison, Bonhoeffer wrote a poem called "Who Am I?" In it, he said he had often been told how brave he was, what a cheerful spirit he had in spite of his imprisonment and hardships, how friendly he was even to his captors, how well he bore his days of misfortune "so smilingly and proudly like one accustomed to win." Yet, he goes on to say, "Am I then really that which other men tell of? Or am I only what I myself know of myself?" He then speaks of his own weakness, his restlessness in prison, his longing to be free, his yearning for colors, for flowers, for the voices of birds. He winds up with:

> Who am I? This or the other?
> Am I one person today and tomorrow another?
> Am I both at once? A hypocrite before others, and
>   before myself a contemptible woebegone
>   weakling?
> Or is something within me still like a beaten army
>   fleeing in disorder from victory already
>   achieved?
> Who am I? They mock me, these lonely questions
>   of mine.
> Whoever I am, Thou knowest, O God, I am thine![26]

That's where I relate to Bonhoeffer, not as the mighty man of God he unquestionably was, but as a struggling human being, struggling to put on a front of strength and piety and Christian virtue. I am keenly aware of my great weaknesses, my hurts, my longing for what I don't have and yet so desperately want—wanting to have it all put together. There are still so many pieces missing and out of place in the jigsaw puzzle that is my life.

Yet, through it all, I know there is one who does have all the pieces of the puzzle in his hand, who sees my weakness as he has seen weakness in thousands upon thousands of men and women down through the centuries and who says to me, as he said to them, "My strength is made perfect in weakness" (2 Corinthians 12:9, KJV). He can take our weakness if we give it to him and turn it into a strength that will redound to his glory and our benefit. People will know it is he who came to our rescue.

Dietrich Bonhoeffer, I'm with you. I know where you're coming from. I'm there too.

31

Each Person Has a Breaking Point

Each of us has a breaking point. Every person is vulnerable to a straw, or a ton of hay, that can break a camel's back, or his or her own. We may be able to take just so much, and then that extra added event comes along that can make us collapse, even at a time when we think we're doing well.

Some people seem to breeze through life; nothing seems to faze them. They often appear to go from victory to victory and get just about anything they want—financially, emotionally, or any other way. They never seem to collapse or crumble.

But I wonder just how much they could take if that wonderful world started to come apart at the seams. Suppose they lost a piece of it, a major piece, then another, then another. Somewhere along the line I think they would crack, would come to the end of their rope. I don't think any of us is immune to cracking. Some may have a higher breaking point than others. It may take ten catastrophes to break these people, while for some of us it may take only one or two. But I don't think there's a person alive who can truthfully say, "I'd *never* break."

I've always been skeptical of those who criticized a prisoner of war for breaking under torture and giving away secrets, when they had never encountered any torture themselves. I mentioned in the last chapter the movie in which a prisoner was made to talk by having bamboo sticks pushed up under his fingernails and lit.

But as bad as physical torture is, in many ways I believe emotional torture is just as devastating. A broken heart can destroy a person in a way no broken bone can. Subjecting someone to loneliness is just as cruel as putting him or her on the rack. Twisting someone's life is just as brutal as twisting limbs, especially if we do it consciously.

And I think there's just so much emotional torture we can take before we break. When that point is reached, when one hurt or disappointment is piled on top of another, we're going to feel down—no doubt about it. And whether a person is a Christian doesn't seem to make a difference. Christians aren't immune to hurt and emotional down times. So when these moments come, we are to recognize them for what they are and not feel guilty. The down times won't last, not if we know Jesus Christ. Once we develop a history of having Christ lift us out of these low times, we can wait them out better. We know the sun (the Son too) will rise again because it (he) has in the past.

32

Rights

There is a classic book called *Tracks of a Fellow Struggler*[27] by John Claypool. If you happen to be going through a grief experience, especially the loss of a child, I recommend it highly.

Although the book is about grief, it nevertheless gave me the impetus to write on rights. John Claypool's ten-year-old daughter died of leukemia, and the book is a rewrite of four sermons he preached during the time of her struggle and after her death.

Claypool tells of his own personal struggle, his doubts, even his anger and questioning of God. He tells of several roads out of despair. One he doesn't recommend is silent resignation, a road advised by many of his Christian friends.

One friend who did help him wrote to him that he had no word for the suffering of the innocent and never had had, but "I fall back on the idea that God has a lot to give an account for." This might sound blasphemous to some, and it shocked John Claypool at first, but the more he thought about it, the truer he felt it was to the path of the Bible. He puts it this way:

Words and questions and dialogue . . . are at the
heart of the way persons—especially fathers and
children—ought to relate. Where, then, did we
Christians ever get the notion that we must not
question God or that we have no right to pour out
our souls to him and ask, "Why?"

I, for one, see nothing but a dead end down
this road of silent resignation, for it is one of
those medicines that cures at the expense of
killing the organisms it is supposed to heal. After
all, my questions in the face of this event are a
real part of me just now, and to deny them or
suppress them by bowing mechanically to a
superior Force is an affront, not only to God and
to my nature, but to the kind of relation we are
supposed to have. There is more honest faith in
an act of questioning than in the act of silent sub-
mission, for implicit in the very asking is the
faith that some light can be given.

I am really honoring God when I come clean
and say, "You owe me an explanation." For, you
see, I believe He will be able to give me such an
accounting when all the facts are in, and until
then, it is valid to ask.

It is not rebelliousness, then, but faith that
keeps me from finding any promise down the
road of unquestioning resignation. This approach
is closer to pagan Stoicism than Christian humility. I have no choice but to submit to this event
of death. Still, the questions remain, and I

believe I honor God by continuing to ask and seek and knock, rather than resigning myself like a leaf or rock.

At no point in its [the Bible's] teaching is there ever an indication that God wants us to remain like rocks or even little infants in our relationship to Him. He wants us to become mature sons and daughters, which means that He holds us responsible for our actions and expects us to hold Him responsible for His!

Another dead end is labeling all tragedy "God's will." Claypool says:

I think there is an important lesson for us to learn here about how to help others in the grieving process: it is always futile and unproductive to try to explain tragedy in some comprehensive way. Saying piously that a loss is "the will of God" does not solve anything and may even create a sense of anger in the person who has been hurt. The calamities of life are all deeply mysterious and the more we try to "explain" them to each other and fix the blame and responsibility here or there, the farther we get from the truth. Job's friends, because of their misguided intellectualizing, actually stimulated in him a seething resentment against God and the whole universe. Admittedly, he might have come to this position on his own, but there is no doubt he was driven forward by his friends.

I have had well-meaning people tell me to accept my divorce as "God's will." I too almost felt the "seething resentment against God" that John Claypool describes. I felt resentment against a God who would "will" such a tragedy. Frustration and despair come from a feeling of "even God doesn't understand. Even God won't lift a finger to right the wrong." But the resentment vanished when the advice was discounted and I knew in my heart of hearts that God is consistent, that he would never will anything that goes against his expressed word. The God I know and love isn't like that.

The third road out of despair, the one Dr. Claypool took and the one I'm trying to get on, is the realization that we have no right to happiness or to be free of tragedy. In the story of Job, God had to remind him that the things he had become so indignant about losing actually did not belong to him in the first place. To quote Claypool:

> They were gifts—gifts beyond his deserving, graciously given him by Another, and thus not to be possessed or held onto as if they were his. To be angry because a gift has been taken away is to miss the whole point of life. That we ever have the things we cherish is more than we deserve. Gratitude and humility rather than resentment should characterize our handling of the objects of life.
>
> Life, too, is a gift, and it is to be received and participated in and handled with gratitude. . . .

Only when life is seen as a gift and received with the open hands of gratitude is it the joy God meant for it to be.

There's the key. There's the helpful insight. It's our attitude toward life that counts. Do we look on it as our baby, our ballpark, an arena in which we have a right to all the goodies? How different all this would be if we took the attitude John Claypool recommends, if we looked at life as a gift instead of a right.

I once attended a class in which *The Great Divorce*[28] by C. S. Lewis was being discussed. The teacher asked the class to name all the rights we felt we were entitled to. After reviewing the rather long list, the teacher made a startling statement: In *The Great Divorce* C. S. Lewis was saying that none of these rights was valid, that we have absolutely no rights. Life is a gift, and our attitude is to be grateful and thankful for what we have, not bitter and demanding over we what we don't. If we all took that attitude (and I include myself as an offender), how differently life might evolve.

No silent resignation is called for. A dialogue with God, even a questioning of him is permissible, sometimes desirable. Yet in the final analysis we must realize that if we are going to move on through the valley to the plains and mountaintops, we have no basic right to anything. If we can refocus our eyes and hearts so that we look to God with gratitude instead of bitterness, with humility instead of arrogance, with a willingness to obey instead of a tendency to make excuses for not doing so, then I believe many of the things that upset or destroy us will lose their power over us. The poison of hate and despair will be transformed into a balm of love and peace.

A dear friend wrote to me while I was in a time of despair:

> When something is ending, something else is beginning. Endings do close the doors on chapters of our lives, but it does always mean the beginning of something else. We wish you great beginnings and pray for the best chapter yet of your life to begin.

If I can look forward to that chapter with anticipation and not with a demand for my rights, I'll have a much better chance of achieving what this friend hopes for me. But don't ever let me leave you with the impression it's easy. It most certainly is not! It *is* possible, though, and that's enough to live on.

33

Major Disappointments

No one goes through life without suffering major disappointments. But perhaps we should define what we mean by major disappointments. Unrequited love could certainly be classified as major. Even a twelve-year-old involved in the first pangs of puppy love feels the pain of unreturned love. And then as we grow older that pain seems intensified, or at least longer lasting, when someone fails to respond. I've experienced unrequited love. I can vouch for the fact that it's painful. A career setback, unemployment, failure to achieve our youthful goals can be major disappointments. I've experienced those too.

Then there's the death of a child. I haven't experienced that, but I know it must be horrible. To call that a "major disappointment" is indeed an understatement. Maybe "crushing blow" would be a better term.

In the late 1970s I was intrigued to read a comment by a man on the Washington scene about some of former president Jimmy Carter's advisors. He thought they were too young and inexperienced. But his most interesting statement was, "No one should serve [in a major advisory position] unless he is forty years old and has suffered one major disappointment in life."

I once read an article called "Maturing through Disappointment." The author quoted a statement by Epictetus: "Men are not disturbed by the things that happen, but by their opinion of the things that happen." Then the author added, "This is a setback, I thought. But it is not the end of the world unless I choose to let it be. It is not what has happened to me but what I think about it that can be so devastating."

How much easier said than done! It's easy to say, "Think positively," but it's so hard to do it when our whole world is collapsing about us, when we're suffering one major disappointment after another. I can't say that I've learned yet to be a "positive thinker." No, my way to handle major disappointments is to be a *Christ* thinker. If I can get my thoughts on him, I'll be okay. If I dwell on the major disappointment, I'll dissolve into self-pity and end up on a toboggan going nowhere. If I can remember all that Christ has done for me in the past and look to the future with expectancy, I'll be okay. But if I start to doubt, heaven help me. In fact, only heaven can help me.

I do think, though, we can mature through our disappointments. I wonder how those who sail through life with everything going their way, with no major disappointments, ever develop character. We know how the oyster gets its pearl. It's an irritant placed in the shell that leads to a reaction producing the pearl. This is indeed an apt analogy of some wonderful people I know whose lives have been shaped by their reactions to major disappointments.

A major disappointment will either crush us or make us. We can start feeling sorry for ourselves, start hitting the bottle, engage in promiscuous sexual activity, or strike out in any of a half-dozen or more directions in an attempt (always a vain one) to kill the pain. But morning always comes, and we have to face it.

Or we can turn to Christ. He won't take all the pain away, at least not overnight. But he'll comfort us enough so we can bear it. This belief does not come out of some personal theory but out of personal experience. I know this because God's healing is working in me as I write these lines.

My purpose in sharing this with you is to encourage anyone who may be suffering major disappointments at this moment. Believe me, there can be a positive side to the situation, as much as we may believe that isn't possible. We have a choice—self-pity or a total commitment of our lives to Jesus Christ and the laying of all our burdens on the one who said, "I will never leave you or forsake you." He *won't*. Believe me, he won't.

34

Failure

Failure. What an ugly word! What an ugly life position to be in.

In a TV interview, actor Jack Lemmon said, "Failure doesn't mean a thing. It's not going to hurt to fail. I've learned as much from failure as any success I've had." Although I *do* think it hurts to fail, I think it's true that we can learn as much from failure as from success. In fact, I think failure can teach us a lot more than success can.

I believe there's a big difference between *fail* and *failure.* Many of us fail at one time or other. Some of us fail many times. But that doesn't make us failures. Failure sounds so final. It sounds as if it's all over—no more chances.

I once met a harried woman in an airport who was really down in the dumps. She confided to me with exhaustive detail her litany of failures. Because of some past experiences I had had, I was able to tell her in all honesty, "You may have failed, but you're not a failure."

At one time in my life I was convinced I was a

failure. I thought it was all over—no hope, no future, nothing left to live for. Then I met a man who helped turn it all around for me. Like the woman in the airport, I told him I was a failure. He replied, "How can you say you're a failure? You have a great attribute. You have the capability to love deeply. Any person who can do that is not a failure."

Before that incident I had frequently expressed my feelings of failure but inevitably received the response: "It's all your fault," "You have a lousy attitude," "Get off your duff and go do something for somebody else," and all the other cliches that really don't help a person in deep trouble. All they did was drive me into deeper despair.

But the fact that my new friend saw something good in me, something positive, began to give me a new lease on life. I could begin to believe I was worth something. I could begin to understand that, even though I failed once in a while, I wasn't a failure.

Smiley Blanton, a well-known Christian psychiatrist, wrote a book called *Love or Perish*[29] in which he claimed that unless we are loved and can love, we will perish, actually die—physically or emotionally, or both. He had some interesting statistics to back this up. He found that a number of young children deprived of love actually did die. And there's no telling how many adults have died prematurely because no one loved them or because they had no one to love.

The friend who helped me turn my life around by assuring me I wasn't a failure is one of the kindest, most loving men I've ever known. But in a sense he was a stand-in for the real love that came into my life. He was a surrogate, standing in the breach and offering love until I was able to discover the Christ who had brought genuine love into his life and who would eventually bring it into mine. In Christ's eyes, none of us is a failure. He knows that we fail from time to time, but with his help and his love we can turn any failure into a blazing success.

35

Don't Ever Give Up

A man who had spent most of his life in prison for a crime he didn't commit maintained his innocence all those years. When he was finally cleared, to encourage others he said: "Don't ever give up hope. Stand up for your rights. Fight for your rights."

In this connection, let me quote Paul Tournier from his book, *The Strong and the Weak:*

> In the light of the Bible, our life is seen as a gift from God, an incomparable treasure, entrusted by him to us, a talent which we must put to use and protect, so that it may bear fruit. To let ourselves be crushed, to allow the aspirations which God has put in our hearts to be stifled, to keep our convictions to ourselves, to abdicate our own personality, to allow someone else to substitute his tastes, his will, and his ideas for ours—that would be to bury our talent in the ground like the servant in the parable. That would be to disobey God.[30]

I think Dr. Tournier and the released prisoner are saying basically the same thing. But as a Christian, I would have worded the prisoner's admonition a little differently. He said stand up for *your* rights. It would be better said, "Stand up for what *is* right." There is ample biblical justification for that—for standing firm for what is right in the face of all kinds of opposition.

As with so many issues in life, there is a fine line here. There may be some deluded people who are convinced they are right about a cause or a matter and would take Tournier's counsel as justification to try to shout down other persons they feel are wrong. So Tournier has an absolute standard that removes many matters of contention from the subjective to the objective realm. That absolute standard is the Bible. If the Bible backs us up, if Jesus Christ's words back us up, then we can stand up boldly for what it says, for what is right.

I don't think there is anything worse or sadder than a crushed Christian (and I was one myself once, so I know what it's like). This is a Christian who has given up on life, one who has allowed another human being to so control him or her that feeling worthless is the result.

Until recently I hadn't come to terms with the idea that being a crushed Christian is, in a real sense, disobeying God, just like the servant in Jesus' parable who buried his talent in the ground. It is a form of mocking God—taking one of his beautiful gifts, rejecting it, saying that it is worthless, that God has no power to work with it, to transform it into something of joy and beauty.

We must never give up on the power of God to transform a human life, even our own. We must never sell ourselves or the power of the Gospel short. To abdicate our personality, to fail to stand up for what is right after searching God's Word for an answer is, in reality, selling God short. I know of a particular Christian who once did that, who sold himself short in every way. Yet after he had completely committed his life to Jesus Christ, and after God's spirit had come into that life and literally performed miracles, someone said to him, "You always seem as if you're excited by life." He is. I am that man!

36

Something
to Hope For

Tom Landry, former coach of the Dallas Cowboys, has a prescription for a happy life: "Something to hope for, something to do, someone to love." I'd like to look at the first of these: something to hope for. I think that in Christian circles too much emphasis is laid on living in the here and now. We aren't supposed to look toward the future, except the future in the next life. We aren't good Christians unless we are, as the Apostle Paul put it, "content in the state I am in." So we fake it and say we are content, just so we will be accepted. We even brainwash ourselves into thinking we are.

I have felt (or at least honestly thought I felt) totally content in a particular state. But I'm not sure I was being realistic. I'm not sure the human condition allows us to be in a state without hope for change or betterment. I'm not sure it would be healthy. The hopeless inmates of mental institutions typify those living in the present with no hope or anticipation for a better or brighter future.

Viktor Frankl, in his book *The Doctor and the Soul,*[31] tells of his experience in a concentration camp during the Second World War: The inmates who gave up hope were the ones who died—physically or emotionally, or both. From this Dr. Frankl learned that a person can't really exist without a fixed point in the future. When a person loses a future, he or she may be overcome by that sense of emptiness and meaninglessness often affecting the unemployed. Frankl says, "Healthy living is living with an eye on the future."

We don't have to look forward to big things. I have a friend who says we need to look forward to *something*. Many people like to go shopping. Perhaps that's psychologically related to the human need to look forward to something exciting and new.

We can so easily get in a rut. Our world can become humdrum. But let's dare to hope, to look forward to something, and not feel guilty about it. It's a human need. Jesus told us not to be anxious about the future. I don't think he told us not to think about it or look forward to it. After all, he said he came to bring us the abundant life. Isn't that worth getting excited about and looking forward to?

37

Through the Eyes of Faith

Os Guinness in his scholarly work *The Dust of Death*[32] says: "A viewpoint is important because it determines what one sees, not necessarily what there is to be seen."

How true. What we want or expect to see colors what we actually do see.

In C. S. Lewis' *The Magician's Nephew*[33] there is a magnificent scene in which the country of Narnia is created. This is very analogous to biblical accounts of the creation of earth except that in *The Magician's Nephew*, the Christ figure, Aslan, *sings* the world into being rather than speaking as God did. There are several characters present when this takes place. One, a cab driver from London who has been transported out of this world by magic, is very interested in watching and listening to what is going on. He sees and hears so much more because he is paying strict attention. He is viewing creation with the eyes of faith, so to speak, and because of that absorbs vastly more than some of the other characters. For example, the evil magician, Andrew, who is very bored with the creation, misses out on some significant happenings. He is no better off at the end of the book than he was at the beginning—still evil, still absorbed in his own pleasures and machinations. The cabby, however, ends up as the first King of Narnia.

I see two applications of what Os Guinness has said about our viewpoint determining what we actually do see and in what C. S. Lewis has depicted in his novel. First, if we are seeking Christ with eyes of faith, we will see him. Not many of us actually see his physical presence. Not many of us have visions. But I don't know of anyone who has earnestly sought him who hasn't seen him. He promised us that. He promised us that anyone who diligently sought him would find him. But while it may appear that we are the searchers and that he may even be hiding, I don't think it actually works that way. When the truth ultimately is known, I think we'll find he has been the seeker and we the sought; he, the Good Shepherd in search of his lost lambs, has been standing at the door of our hearts knocking and waiting patiently to be let in.

When we are looking and seeing with eyes of faith, somehow we get a perspective on life that those who aren't looking never see. Things fall into place. There's a discernable rhyme and reason to events. I can't explain this at all well to people who aren't looking, but those who see with the eyes of faith will know what I'm talking about. We don't see everything clearly. We still "see through a glass darkly." We still can't explain some of the tragedies that happen in life. But, in general, we stop questioning because of our trust. And we trust because the object of our trust has proven himself trustworthy time and time again.

There's a second aspect, though, of what Guinness is talking about, and it's this. If we already have our minds made up about something or someone, we are going to see exactly what we've already prejudged. If we've already written someone off as no good or unlovable, then whatever he or she does is going to be seen as unworthy. If we say, "I don't love him," then we won't. There's no way we can.

On the other hand, if we are open to the good in others, if we are actually trying to find what that good is so we can affirm it, we will be able to find it. All of us have some good in us, just as we all have imperfections. If we want to try to find those character blemishes and concentrate on them and write somebody off because of them, we'll be most successful. I don't know of a person in whom we couldn't find at least some bad if we looked for it. But why try? How pointless! Doesn't it make more sense to look for the good? Guinness is so right. Our viewpoint is what is so important, so crucial. It does determine what we see, not necessarily what there is to be seen.

38

Mid-Life Crisis

I once read an article in my old hometown paper about four people who had changed careers in mid-life. All of them were in their forties and fifties, and some of them were successful by the world's standards. Two were teachers; one at age fifty-three had gone from a vice president of marketing position with a printing company to a graduate teaching post in English at a local university. Although his financial reward was greatly reduced, he and his wife had adjusted, and the other rewards more than made up for it. He had started to find some meaning in his life that a big income didn't provide.

Then I heard of an old acquaintance who had reached the top of the corporate ladder as the relatively young president of his family business. His income was substantial, he had a lovely wife and a beautiful home; but that wasn't enough—he said his life lacked meaning. In this instance my friend's search did not lead him to another job but to a discovery of Jesus Christ and a life commitment to him. He even began taking a course at a local seminary on witnessing so he would be better able to share his faith.

I have another high school friend who is a minister and teacher of religion at an eastern university. He sent me a paper he had written on anxiety. His thesis is that the type of anxiety people experience varies to some extent with the social and income class in which they find themselves. He maintains that the upper classes, those with plenty of money, frequently experience anxiety because their lives have no meaning. Obviously, not all corporate executives or affluent people experience this type of anxiety, but he felt it was a rather frequent occurrence—one we can see if we just look around us or even look inside of ourselves. The point he was making was that even though there may be no pressure to have enough bread on the table, there is still an anxiety to be felt if life lacks real meaning.

One Christmas I visited the town in which I grew up. While there I heard of three marriages that had failed and of a fourth one that was very shaky—all in extremely well-to-do families. Three of the men were millionaires, and the fourth was a very successful businessman with a prestigious company. What happened? I don't know, but I strongly suspect that the thesis of my minister friend was proved again. While they had millions of dollars, highly successful careers, sumptuous homes, and all the amenities of life, their lives had lost all sense of meaning and direction.

I can identify with that. At one time my life had lost all sense of meaning. The relatively successful career and moderate affluence that marked my experience at mid-life was in reality, as Pascal described it, a "God-shaped vacuum" that only Jesus Christ could fill. And without that vacuum being filled, without a personal relationship with Christ, there will always be an uneasiness, an anxiety, that dollars and successful careers won't satisfy. I think God created us this way so we would seek him out in an attempt to have true meaning in our lives.

39

Does It Hurt to Be a Christian?

In *The Horse and His Boy*[34] by C. S. Lewis, Aslan, the great lion, scratches Aravis. He doesn't tell her he has scratched her as punishment for something she had done to her slave girl. No, he says he scratched her because "you need to know what it felt like."

What's Lewis getting at here? When we get in close to Aslan (or Christ), what's going to happen to us? We're going to see ourselves as we are, end up more sensitive to others, and have a compassion we've never felt before. In the process of gaining that compassion we often have to be hurt ourselves. In the very first chapter I mentioned the phrase "wounded healer," meaning we have to be "wounded" ourselves before we can be used to help heal others.

Aravis needed to know how the slave girl felt; then began the growing awareness of what she had done to somebody else. As Earl Palmer, a Presbyterian pastor, puts it:

When you get in close to the Gospel, you begin

to get a . . . crystal clear look at yourself; and you begin to see some of the beatings that the people around you are taking. It really begins to hurt. As you discover Christ's love you begin to hurt because you've become sensitive. That's the conviction of the Holy Spirit that enables us to see our sins.

John Newton, who wrote the immortal hymn "Amazing Grace," was converted when he began to feel for the slaves down in the hold of the slave ship he was piloting. Again to quote Earl Palmer:

Aslan (Christ) scratched John Newton's back, and he began to feel what those people down in the hold of the ship were feeling. That's a painful experience. A lot of people shy away from the Christian faith for that reason alone. They are not about to have to come to the point where you see who you are and see what you've done, not as punishment but as part of redemption.

Those of us who have come close to Christ will understand what Lewis is saying. We have had our backs (and our hearts) scratched. And very possibly it was our Aslan who scratched, or allowed the scratching, so we could hurt enough to feel what we were doing to others by our selfishness and self-centeredness.

In the story, Aravis becomes a whole new person. She evidences real concern for the slave girl, which is proof that redemption has done its work in her—even as it will in us as we are scratched and brought into a personal relationship with Jesus Christ. His healing love is the balm that eases the pain of life's hurts, and gives a joy and purpose we could never have without him.

40

The Mark of
Inner Healing

In *The Adventure of Living* Paul Tournier insists that
an authentic experience of Christian conversion leads a
person into a great spiritual adventure. The "routine of
religion" becomes an "adventure of religion." However,
even in the face of this adventure possibility, Tournier
goes on to admit that "man is capable of spoiling his
life." And he recounts the despair that is expressed often
in the intimacy of his counseling room, as people con-
fess to the mess they have made of their lives—here are
relived the tragic errors and lost opportunities of the
past, the consequences of which cannot be escaped.

But the good news that Dr. Tournier has for these
people is that "life is not yet over." And he gives a beautiful example in the life of Suzanne Fouche, a woman
who was struck down in the prime of her life by disease
and infirmity. From her own experience she has learned
what new energies can spring to life in a human who
fights for social reintegration. Tournier says:

From her own experience she learned that [her]

disability, far from being an insurmountable obstacle, can be the starting point of a great adventure, of fulfillment and success, provided they [people with disabilities] are given practical assistance to make readaptation possible, and real fellowship to sustain their enthusiasm.[35]

Fouche went on to found and direct an organization in France offering the disabled the instruction and training they need in order to enter a career that is more useful than the one they had to give up because of their disability. Her goal was to enable these people to eventually be able to say to themselves, "I should not have lived such a successful life if I had not been disabled."

John Calvin once said a similar thing. He wrote an invalid that it was difficult to lend an ear to God amidst the honors and riches and influences of the world. He told him: "God has willed to take you aside, as it were, so as to be heard more clearly. He has given you this opportunity to profit in His school, as if He wanted to speak to you privately in your ear."

The disability need not be merely physical. Some of the most excruciating of all disabilities are emotional— the feeling that "I've blown it," "I've missed the golden opportunities that come but once," "I'm a failure when I had a chance to be a success." I know this is true. I have experienced those feelings myself. I've felt them in my innermost being.

But I can also witness to the fact that healing is taking place in my life because I now believe that if it hadn't been for the disability, for the lost opportunities, I would never have had the joy of a personal relationship with Jesus Christ. I now see that the pain and suffering have been worthwhile because this led me to an experience with him I would never have had otherwise. I can honestly say that if I could relive my life, I wouldn't change the direction, even though it has involved suffering and disappointment and even though it has been something less than the successful life another direction offered.

It is true I haven't always felt that way. I agonized for years over a choice I felt was wrong. It almost ruined my life. But now I have come to understand just a little bit of what Jesus meant when he said, "For what will it profit them if they gain the whole world but forfeit their life?" (or miss a chance for the joy and adventure of a personal relationship with him).

I believe that true inner healing comes when we can honestly say that we wouldn't trade our position in Christ for anything else the world has to offer. Or as Suzanne Fouche puts it, "I should not have lived such a successful life if I had not been disabled." This is authentic inner healing, and there is only one physician—Jesus Christ—who can heal in that manner, who can bind up the deepest wounds of the soul and make it whole again.

41

Can Reality
Be Altered?

Charles Colson, renowned for his association with former U.S. president Richard Nixon, credits a major part of his conversion and understanding of it to the book *Mere Christianity* by C. S. Lewis. It was given to him by a friend, then the president of Raytheon Corporation, who himself had recently committed his life to Christ. It was the change and new life in this man that first piqued Colson's interest in the possibility of a change in his own life as well. Colson writes:

> I opened *Mere Christianity* and found myself face-to-face with an intellect so disciplined, so lucid, so relentlessly logical that I could only be grateful I had never faced him in a court of law. Soon I had covered two pages of yellow paper with *pros* to my query "Is there a God?" [36]

Charles Colson made a thorough study of the book, using his legal skills to try to determine if there really was such a thing or person as God, and if Jesus Christ was truly who he claimed to be, i.e., God incarnate in human flesh. Colson determined the claims were valid, and he credits Lewis' brilliant intellect for answering his doubts—proof that reality can be altered.

But to fully grasp what is meant by reality, it will be helpful for us to understand that there are two kinds. For example, there are certain God-made laws and truths on which this universe is established. One of these is the law of gravity. We all know a rock thrown up in the air will drop back down immediately. Then there are spiritual laws and truths. Justice is one of these. We worship a just God. When Jesus was walking this earth, he told us that he was committed to justice. And reality or truth is that when we don't obey God, when we disobey truth, we become slaves to the idols of fame or fortune or self-interest, and these idols will ultimately destroy us. The terrible result of being enslaved to sin is that it will destroy us.

But there is a deeper reality, and it is called grace. God has the power to reclaim us from our sin and idolatry and bring us into his kingdom. While most Christians will acknowledge that he can do that—*has* done that through the sacrificial death of Christ on the cross for our ultimate salvation—I believe far too many of us fail to realize that this reclaiming power, this grace is at work in our present lives as well. Even the reality of a selfish disposition or a broken relationship can be changed through the coming of Christ into our lives and the indwelling presence of his Holy Spirit. He can and will change and transform the reality of who and what we are.

So, can reality be altered? Yes! It certainly can, as we confront the reality of who and what we are, how helpless we are to change that reality on our own, and ask for help from the God of change.

42

Past—That's
What the Word Means

There is a classic line in the Pulitzer-prize winning musical *A Chorus Line*. The plot centers around the selection process of a chorus line for a Broadway show. There are only eight spots open, but there are twenty or thirty applicants. The director, as a help in his selection process, asks each one of the applicants to step forward and tell a little of his or her life story.

One young dancer, Paul, has an intense and tragic story to tell. (The actor who played this part won a Tony award for best performance by a featured actor in a musical play. I can understand why.) After the young man has told his sordid story, the director, who hasn't been too compassionate with some of the other candidates, tries to reassure him by saying of his past, "That's what the word means—past." In other words, what went on before is all over now. It isn't the present, and it certainly doesn't have to be the future.

How marvelous that in life the past can be just that. The word *past* does mean something that is over; we need not return to it unless we choose to. I know from experience that the past can continue to haunt us into the present and darken our hopes about the future. But it needn't be that way. We can have a future and a present, too, without the crippling effects of the past.

Before we can do that, though, I think two things must happen. First—and while this may sound like an oversimplification, I think it is not—we must let the past be the past. We must realize, as the director put it, "That's what the word means."

Thank goodness we live in a world where time exists, where the past can be a past. I'm not sure it's always going to be like that. It's beyond my brain to grasp the concept of eternity, where there is only the present, where time as we know it is nonexistent. But for now on earth there is a past, present, and future. Before we can truly live in the present and future, we must let go of the past. Yes, it's easier said than done, and there's no foolproof way of going about it. But I do know the director's advice to young Paul was sound. He had to come to grips with "what's done is done," spilled milk is spilled milk. Part of the real cure comes from saying, "Okay, that is the past, but thank God there's a future as well."

The second thing that must happen is that we come to the knowledge that our future is in the hands of a loving and caring God who will act in our lives if we but ask him and let him. The theologies of those who don't see God acting in a personal way in our lives are of no help. What good does it do to have a God out there somewhere (even a God you may believe in) if he doesn't act? Who could love a God like that? I couldn't.

The God that I know, as he is revealed to me in Jesus Christ, is the kind of God I can and do love. He is the kind of God who can take a broken past and turn even that into a hope for the future. And I'm not just thinking about a future in some kind of heaven, but one on this earth, in this body. Without that, the advice the director gave to the young dancer is only half good. It's fine to say the word *past* means just that. But how much better and more helpful it would have been to be able to say to him (from experience), "Paul, not only is the past behind you, but you can have a joyful future, which the past cannot contaminate, if you will put your trust in Jesus Christ." Psalm 30:5 NRSV illustrates this point: "Weeping may linger for the night, but joy comes with the morning".

Epilogue
Take Off the Black Robe

Perhaps the best way to end a book on Christian encouragement is to talk about what encourages us most. I think it is acceptance—acceptance just as we are.

I once read in a newspaper article the following statement: "It is very important to surround yourself with people who value you." Joseph Venema taught the following in a counseling class at Hollywood Presbyterian Church:

People don't change by being put down or evaluated. People change by being accepted.

People change when they have the freedom to explore and discover who they are. When we are accepted, we don't have to pretend to be righteous. We can then look at all the things we need to be forgiven for. When we are unforgiven, we can't face this. We become too self-defensive. We need to be accepted in spite of our sins.

Judgment does not change people. Take off the black robe and get out of the role of a judge. Deal with what is rather than what ought to be. Work towards acceptance rather than approval.

Be *beside* the other person rather than on top of him. Acceptance is a suspension of judgment.

Let's treat other human beings the same way God treats us. God is the master psychologist. He knows we *can* change. We can change from a life of self-centeredness and selfishness to one centered on him, a life full of joy and purpose and meaning. But *how* does God change us?

God doesn't change us by judging and condemning us. He certainly doesn't change us by turning his back on us. He changes us by loving and accepting us. Once we feel the freedom and safety of his love, once we feel unconditional acceptance that comes from being valued for who we *are* rather than what we do, the catalyst for change has been instilled in our hearts and minds and spirits. God doesn't need to judge us because we will judge *ourselves*. We will feel the conviction of our sin and the motivation to try turning our lives around. We will reach out to him for his help in doing it. But if he first backed us into a corner and lashed out at us, we would probably be so self-defensive we never would change.

One last note of encouragement: You are loved unconditionally. You are loved with a power that can take a broken and sinful life and turn it into a glorious and radiant adventure with Jesus Christ. You are accepted for who you are, not what you do. If you can accept yourself, you can grow.

My hope for you is that you will become the person

God created you to be, that you will feel the joy that comes from being a son or daughter of the King. The Good News of God's love is for you! All you have to do is believe it and accept it.

Notes

Prologue
1. C. S. Lewis, *The Lion, the Witch, and the Wardrobe* (New York: Macmillan, 1952), 76.

Chapter 1
2. Thomas A. Harris, *I'm OK—You're OK* (New York: Harper & Row, 1967).

Chapter 5
3. Joseph Murphy, *The Power of Your Subconscious Mind* (Englewood Cliffs, NJ: Prentice-Hall, 1963), 38.
4. C. S. Lewis, *The Screwtape Letters* (New York: Macmillan, 1959), 59.

Chapter 6
5. John Powell, *Why Am I Afraid to Tell You Who I Am?* (Niles, IL: Argus Communications, 1969).

Chapter 7
6. Clark Barshinger, "Intimacy and Spiritual Growth", *Bulletin of the Christian Association for Psychological Studies*, Vol. 3, No. 2, 1977.

Chapter 10
7. William Glasser, *Reality Therapy* (New York: Harper & Row, 1965).
8. Paul Tournier, *Escape from Loneliness* (Philadelphia: Westminster Press, 1952), 170.

Chapter 11
9. C. S. Lewis, *Letters of C. S. Lewis* (New York: Harcourt Brace Jovanovich, 1966), 155.
10. Paul Tournier, *A Place for You* (New York: Harper & Row, 1968).

11. Gary Collins, *The Christian Psychology of Paul Tournier* (Grand Rapids, MI: Baker Book House, 1973).

Chapter 12
12. Milton Meyerhoff, *On Caring* (New York: Harper & Row, 1968).

Chapter 13
13. Sidney M. Jourard, *The Transparent Self* (New York: D. Van Nostrand, 1971), 93-94, 97-98, 99-100.

Chapter 14
14. George E. Vaillant, *Adaptation to Life* (Boston: Little, Brown, and Co., 1977).
15. Carl Rogers, "From Heart to Heart," *Marriage Encounter,* February 1978.

Chapter 15
16. Vaillant, *Adaptation to Life.*

Chapter 18
17. Elizabeth O'Connor, *Journey Inward—Journey Outward* (New York: Harper & Row, 1968).

Chapter 19
18. C. S. Lewis, *The Voyage of the Dawn Treader* (New York: Macmillan, 1952), 132.

Chapter 20
19. Tournier, *A Place for You.*

Chapter 22
20. Ray Stedman, *Body Life* (Glendale, CA: Regal Books, 1972).

Chapter 23
21. Paul Tournier, *The Strong and the Weak* (Philadelphia: Westminster Press, 1963), 93.

22. Paul Tournier, *To Understand Each Other* (Atlanta: John Knox Press, 1967), 29-30.

Chapter 26

23. C. S. Lewis, *The Four Loves* (New York: Harcourt Brace Jovanovich, 1971).

Chapter 27

24. Ray Stedman, *Authentic Christianity* (Waco, TX: Word Books, 1975).

25. Dietrich Bonhoeffer, *Life Together* (New York: Harper & Row, 1954), 22-23.

Chapter 30

26. Dietrich Bonhoeffer, *The Cost of Discipleship* (New York: Macmillan, 1959), 18.

Chapter 32

27. John Claypool, *Tracks of a Fellow Struggler* (Waco, TX: Word Books, 1974).

28. C. S. Lewis, *The Great Divorce* (New York: Collier Books, McMillan Publishing Company, 1946).

Chapter 34

29. Smiley Blanton, *Love or Perish* (New York: Fawcett World Library, 1971).

Chapter 35

30. Tournier, *The Strong and the Weak*, 184-185.

Chapter 36

31. Viktor Frankl, *The Doctor and the Soul: From Psychotherapy to Logotherapy* (New York: Random House, 1973).

Chapter 37

32. Os Guinness, *The Dust of Death* (Downers Grove, IL: InterVarsity Press, 1973).

33. C. S. Lewis, *The Magician's Nephew* (New York: Macmillan, 1970).

Chapter 39
34. C. S. Lewis, *The Horse and His Boy* (New York: Macmillan, 1970).

Chapter 40
35. Paul Tournier, *The Adventure of Living* (New York: Harper & Row, 1965), 102.

Chapter 41
36. Charles W. Colson, *Born Again* (Lincoln, VA: Chosen Books, 1976), 121.

About Stephen Ministries

Since 1975 Stephen Ministries, a not-for-profit Christian training organization based in St. Louis, Missouri, has produced high-quality, Christ-centered training and resources used in more than 10,000 congregations and organizations. These resources include:

- *Stephen Ministry*—a complete system for training and organizing lay people to provide one-to-one Christian care to hurting people in and around their congregations.

- *ChristCare Group Ministry*—a complete system of training and resources to help congregations direct and grow a Christ-centered, life-changing small group ministry.

- The *Breakthrough Leadership Conference*—in-depth, systematic training for leaders in congregations, large and small businesses, and other organizations.

- *Journeying through Grief*—a set of four short books to send to grieving people at four crucial times during the first year after a loss, providing care, support, and hope.

- *Don't Sing Songs to a Heavy Heart*—a practical book of well-researched ideas for what to say or do (and what *not* to say or do) to offer Christ's loving care to hurting people.

- *Care Classics* like this one, and many other resources.

To learn more about these and other resources, contact:

 Stephen Ministries
2045 Innerbelt Business Center Drive
St. Louis, Missouri 63114-5765
(314) 428-2600
www.stephenministries.org